BUS

CHILDREN
AT WORK

CHILDREN AT WORK

Child Labor Practices in Africa

Anne Kielland & Maurizia Tovo

LYNNE
RIENNER
PUBLISHERS

BOULDER
LONDON

Published in the United States of America in 2006 by
Lynne Rienner Publishers, Inc.
1800 30th Street, Boulder, Colorado 80301
www.rienner.com

and in the United Kingdom by
Lynne Rienner Publishers, Inc.
3 Henrietta Street, Covent Garden, London WC2E 8LU

Library of Congress Cataloging-in-Publication Data
Kielland, Anne.
    Children at work : child labor practices in Africa / Anne Kielland and Maurizia Tovo.
        p. cm.
    Includes bibliographical references and index.
    ISBN 1-58826-409-2 (hardcover : alk. paper)—ISBN 1-58826-433-5 (pbk. : alk. paper)
    1. Child labor—Africa. 2. Child welfare—Africa. 3. Children's rights—Africa. 4.
Child abuse—Africa. 5. Children—Africa—Social conditions. I. Tovo, Maurizia C. II. Title.
HD6250.A352K54 2006
331.3'1096—dc22

                                                                            2005029746

British Cataloguing in Publication Data
A Cataloguing in Publication record for this book
is available from the British Library.

Printed and bound in the United States of America

5 4 3 2 1

Contents

Tables and Figures

Table

Figures

Preface

IT HAS BEEN SAID THAT WHEN YOU HAVE BEEN IN CHINA FOR A WEEK, you can write a letter home. When you have been in China for a month, you can write an article for a newspaper. When you have been in China for a year, you can write a book. But if you stay there any longer, you will find yourself incapable of writing anything whatsoever. This may very well be our case—the fact that two non-Africans have written a book about African children could be an indication of our relative ignorance. On the other hand, we have spent years working on the issue of child labor and have discovered that there is indeed only a limited understanding of the use of child labor in Africa as a distinct phenomenon, both within and outside the continent. So we decided to put together the pieces of research that we found to be particularly insightful, the books and articles that provided the most vivid pictures, the interviews that moved us most, and the cases where the standard maps to African child labor turned out not to match the terrain at all. We also wanted to go a step further and give child laborers a face, to make sure that the words and numbers would not conceal the people behind them. Therefore, we have included the pictures of many of our young acquaintances.*

*Protecting the dignity of the child is an important and often forgotten part of the responsibility of those who call themselves child rights advocates. Photographing children in an embarrassing or miserable state may increase their feelings of humiliation, and in practice may turn into yet another form of abuse. Most of the children we approached over the years actually did refuse to have their picture taken. We have always respected their decisions, no matter how much we wanted to document their plight.

Trying to understand child labor issues in sub-Saharan Africa took us down a path paved with challenges, surprises, misunderstandings, and practical problems. Why, for instance, do researchers have to struggle to find a systematic relationship between child labor and poverty in so many African studies? Scientific research is meant to provide answers. But with some notable exceptions, research findings on child labor in Africa are often so contradictory, counterintuitive, or contrary to research results from elsewhere that they may deepen the confusion. In many ways, Africa may seem to work by a different logic than other continents, and official definitions of concepts like "child labor" or "child trafficking" tend to be of limited practical use in drawing a research sample or determining the eligibility criteria for targeted interventions. In reality, however, the problem here is not Africa: research in Africa merely helps demonstrate the striking limitations of concepts, theories, and analytical tools that have primarily been developed elsewhere.

To increase the challenge, Africa also offers enormous differences within its borders. With such immense variation, it may seem hopelessly superficial to point to anything at all and say that it is "typically African." Besides, our admitted West African bias may make this book even less suitable for generalizations. So we apologize in advance to all our African readers who might at some point exclaim: "Oh no! Not where I come from!" Then again, many times we have seen our urban African colleagues stare in disbelief at what they found in remote areas of their own countries. And we don't blame them—remote parts of our own countries, Norway and Italy, most likely hide some surprises for us too.

Because we want this book to be accessible, we have tried to steer clear of technical terminology and in-depth academic debates. Perhaps to the frustration of our more sophisticated readers, we have avoided tables almost altogether and kept figures to a minimum. To compensate for this occasional lack, however, endnotes provide additional information on sources, statistics, and more technical issues.

We hope the book will prove useful to a wide audience. For newcomers to child labor issues, it may serve as an introduction. For researchers, it may offer some help in explaining findings by suggesting different ways to interpret statistical results. For child labor specialists, the book should provide references to the key debates on child labor in Africa. We also hope that African readers can find value in our approach to an issue that is so much part of their everyday life. We know that, when close to a situation, most people rarely sit down to reflect on its causes and nature.

*   *   *

This book is dedicated to Odile, Rachel, Fousaini, and all the working children we met while exploring child labor issues in Africa. You will find pictures of them throughout.

It is also dedicated to Martine de Souza and the other African consultants and resource people who helped us—two non-Africans—to interpret and better understand what we saw and heard, and who patiently tried to answer our many questions. We would like to mention Elisée Soumonni, Pierre Jekinnou, Roger Ouensavi, Huguette Akplogan-Dossa, Moussa Amadou, Gilberte Hounsounou, and Bisi Olateru-Olagberi.

We also thank our four reviewers—Florence Baingana, Ebrima Sall, Jens Christopher Andvig, and Kevin Bales—for their excellent advice, useful contributions, and inspiration. Eden Hegwood provided editorial assistance.

The pictures in this book were mainly taken by Anne, with two exceptions: Brian Edwards of True Vision shot the picture of the boy with wounds on his back, shown in Chapter 1; and Giacomo Piroizzi of the United Nations Children's Fund photographed the child combatant shown in Chapter 5. We are also grateful to Geneviève Boko Nadjo of Women in Law and Development in Africa who let us use the poster to illustrate the section on child labor and schooling in Chapter 1. All of the children in the pictures we took gave their permission to be photographed.

Thank you all for your contributions, patience, and guidance!

I

Child Labor in Africa: Where to Start?

THE SUN WAS ALREADY BECOMING HOT, BUT IN THE SHADE OF THE mango tree it still felt cool. Nothing is more pleasant than a morning chat in the shade of a mango tree. We settled down and pulled out our notebooks. Not far from us, on the road, groups of children wearing neat khaki uniforms were walking to school. There is something deeply reassuring about watching children going off to school, especially when they are African children wearing neat khaki uniforms. A feeling that things are as they should be mixes with the hope that Africa will be able to rise to the challenges of the twenty-first century.

But of course we knew better. And our African friends were there to remind us: Yes, those children were going to school in the bright light of the morning, but how many of them had sisters and brothers who were not? How many would be going home to an afternoon of work? How many had gotten up at dawn to tend to animals or fetch water and wood?

The official figures tell the story quite starkly: 51 percent of Africans are, legally speaking, children (that is, they are less than 18 years old); and almost one-third of them (31.9 percent)[1] are economically active, which is the highest rate in the world. However, when one looks closer, the reality of child labor is not nearly as clear-cut. To begin, it's not certain who should really be considered a child. Surely there is universal agreement that the legal age for maturity is 18, but most studies on child labor concentrate on the 7–14 age group, or 10–14, suggesting that work by adolescents should not quite be considered child labor. More important, being economically active is not considered to be the same thing as engaging in child labor. The

International Labour Organization (ILO) defines child labor in accordance with the so-called Minimum Age Convention (no. 138) as:[2]

- For 5- to 11-year-olds: "all children at work in economic activity." ILO does not define household chores in one's own household as being economic activities.
- For 12- to 14-year-olds: "all children at work in economic activity, minus those in light work." Light work is defined as nonhazardous work for up to fourteen hours a week. Hazardous work, in turn, is any activity or occupation that can lead to adverse effects on the child's safety, health, and moral development.
- For 15- to 17-year-olds: "all children in the 'worst forms' of child labor." The *unconditional* worst forms are, according to ILO Convention 182: slavery, trafficking, bondage, serfdom and forced compulsory labor, child soldiering, child prostitution, and use of children in drug smuggling and other criminal activities. In addition comes "work which, by its nature or the circumstances in which it is carried out, is likely to harm the health, safety or morals of children."

With this in mind, it is easy to see why investigating the incidence of child labor in Africa may be a frustrating exercise yielding figures that can be highly misleading for a reader who does not look at the fine print. Estimates of African child labor are based on a variety of different surveys and have several weaknesses. First, the measurements of "work" vary from survey to survey. While some only count remunerated work, others simply ask if the child has worked for at least one hour during the past seven days (or the past two weeks). Still others ask whether a child's main activity is school or work, and some count only out-of-school children as working, ignoring all the children who combine school and work, and including children who are simply idle. In this way, statistics from one country will consider a schoolboy who delivers newspapers the same as a child working in the mines to survive, while statistics from a neighboring country will only count the miners.

To complicate matters further, many surveys don't count domestic work, and consequently the majority of girls' (and women's) labor activities go vastly underrepresented, giving the false impression that boys work much more than girls. Ironically, even the girls themselves tend not to see their household chores as work—actually, it may not occur to them to report these chores at all. Anthropologist Pamela Reynolds found that in the diary notes she collected from rural children in the

Zambezi valley, the boys at times described the domestic work activities of their sisters, while the sisters themselves forgot to mention these activities.[3]

The challenge of accurately measuring African child labor is well illustrated by the different results obtained with different research methods. In 1998 the United Nations Development Programme (UNDP) in Benin carried out a unique time allocation study. While official national statistics reported a child labor participation rate of 27.5 percent, the time allocation study concluded that almost all of the 6- to 14-year-olds in the sample did in fact carry out some sort of work during the twenty-four hours they were under observation. This confirms the perception of most people familiar with African reality: when children work in Africa, it is not the exception but the rule. The real question is not whether chil-

Low levels of mechanization create a high demand for manual labor, for instance in mining. This photograph shows a child miner in Burkina Faso.

Sub-Saharan Africa

Population 620 million

0–18 year olds 318 million

Total fertiltity rate 5.7 (South Asia, 3.5; Latin America, 2.7)

Under-5 mortality rate 175/100,000 (South Asia, 100; Latin America, 37)

GNP per capita $528 (South Asia, $455; Latin American, $3,713)

Life expectancy 48 years (South Asia, 62 years; Latin America, 70 years)

Adult literacy rate 61 percent (South Asia, 53 percent; Latin America,
       88 percent)

---

dren work, but rather how much they work, what they do, in what kind of environment, and in what kind of personal situation.

Africa is poorer, more rural, and less industrialized than other continents. As a global trend, poorer countries tend to have higher rates of child labor because parents cannot afford the cost of schooling—and in some cases the schools are simply not there. It is common to assume that parents would prefer their children to go to school if they could only afford to. Child labor thus appears as a last resort for poor parents, but as we will see, reality may prove to be more complex. Child labor is clearly more common in rural traditional societies around the world, and the fact that Africa is less urbanized than other places makes it a high-risk area. At the same time, the low level of mechanization creates a strong demand for manual labor, which is the type of work children are capable of doing without much training or supervision.

Child Labor as Socialization

It is often claimed that child labor is an age-old way of life in Africa—part of its tradition and culture. However, in terms of child labor practices, Africa has had at least three historical stages of major importance. In the first stage we find the hunter and gatherer societies. These societies were often nomadic and the adults would walk far from the camp searching for food. Children were often not recruited into this subsistence work for two reasons. First, the hunters and gatherers worked less than modern sedentary Africans, and adults could most efficiently do the work. In the game-rich Kalahari, for instance, it was often sufficient for adults to hunt for two or three days a week. Second, bringing children along would simply slow the hunters down. Besides, children under a certain age are poor hunters: they have little patience, are not good at aiming at a distance, and do not have the strength to throw a spear very far.[4] In the nomadic camps there were relatively few tasks to perform, as there were few food production or activities. Research on the !Kung in Botswana concluded that children of hunting and gathering families tended to stay in the camp under the guidance of the elderly and the adults who were not hunting on a given day, that children had a much closer relationship to their parents than they do today, and that the elderly were more available and less distant, since the norms of deference and respect that are so typical in modern sedentary African households did not exist.[5] Moreover, gender roles were much less clearly defined. Children—probably because of the lack of alternatives in the small camp—mostly played with other children of all ages and both genders, and adults did more or less the same type of work. In contrast, the children and parents of sedentary !Kung were less physically proximate, as the parents spent less time in the household and they were mostly occupied with work when they were at home. Unlike for the nomadic !Kung, there were huge differences in playtime between sedentary boys and girls. There were also more obvious gender differences compared to boys and girls in the bush, who tended to play in equal amounts.[6]

This suggests that while considering child labor as a tradition may be correct, we should bear in mind that this tradition may be of a relatively recent date, primarily referring to the second historical stage: settlement and farming. It is often claimed that the exploitative forms of child labor seen in Africa today are some sort of perversion of more socially healthy practices that consolidated in this second period. We believe, however, that this argument is simplistic and reveals a partial ignorance about the role of many children in the sedentary cultures. In many societies, slavery, for instance, was as rampant for children as for adults, and labor conditions for underprivileged children on farms and in households were not likely to have been very idyllic.[7] In this more recent historical stage, two new factors came to strongly influence many traditional African societies: the introduction of Islam and the introduction of Christian colonial rule. While both brought new perspectives on work ethics, the latter also brought and spread the practice of large-scale plantation farming, often for export.[8]

The third historical stage—child labor in the form seen today in

Africa—is a result of the rapid and rather violent encounter between a rural farming society and a modern urban culture. The African farmer families and their production systems appear to have been unprepared to cope with the industrialization, monetarization, materialism, and individualism brought by modernization and urbanization. Over a relatively short time, centuries-old extended family structures have disintegrated and traditional child-fostering arrangements have changed character; this, alongside the introduction of formal education for the lucky, has led to enormous inequalities in the lives of African children, who in the past had fairly homogeneous experiences. While there is no reason to idealize the labor situation of children in earlier history, to some children in this third stage, working stopped being primarily about learning essential life skills and turned into economic exploitation and mere coping.

Which role did work play in child rearing in recent African history? Based on a vast literature on socialization practices in different ethnic groups, Sara Oloko at Harvard University described this role in six points:[9]

1. Since children worked with or for their parents, the latter, within the limits of their knowledge and circumstances, ensured that children's work was appropriate to their capabilities and expected gender role, thus promoting the children's best interests.

2. The division of labor was based on gender and age. In all occupations in which children participated, there was a complementarity of tasks between adults and their children of the same sex. In some trades, children's tasks were so vital that adults' decisions on whether to enter into a particular trade depended on access to children's help. For example, the profitability of the Hausa women's trade in northern Nigeria was reported to vary directly with their utilization of children. Such valued work was perceived as enhancing the self-esteem and self-image of children.

3. The prevalent living arrangement with the extended family provided an important pool of knowledge. In particular, grandparents monitored the activities of children with respect to the timing and the intensity of their involvement in work.

4. There was fusion of work and play, and children anticipated their economic role in early years through role-play. The simplicity of work tools facilitated their use as play items, while singing and dancing during or after work created a positive attitude toward work.

5. The availability of several children within a given age group in an extended family ensured that younger children had ample opportunities to tag along and learn from the older ones who worked. By the time

children began to work on their own, they were able to meet the technical and attitudinal requirements of their tasks, and they knew how to handle work problems. 6. The environment in which children worked was relatively safe, physically and socially. The presence of parents and other friendly adults in the work situation ensured that children were protected in case of threat or danger. More generally, the communities in which children worked were fairly homogeneous settings in which adults had custodial and protective attitudes toward children, even if they were not related to them.

The fact that work was an inherent part of a child's socialization process does not mean that the economic benefits of child labor were just a fortunate by-product. Life was even more labor-demanding in the past and children's contributions were needed. Besides, exploitation is not a new invention, and enslavement—inclusive of children—has existed on the continent at all times. Moreover, the family structure in many African societies was strictly hierarchical, and at times strongly authoritarian. Women were subordinated to their husbands in (often) polygamous families, and favoritism among children was widespread when it came to the allocation of labor. Having a stepparent could have disastrous effects for a child's work life, as being a stepchild meant being at the bottom of the pecking order. Still, the enormous differences found within the same country and even the same household today were nowhere near as evident in the past. Now it is not unusual for a rich urban child to be left to play and study all day within the very same household where the child of a poor rural relative works sixteen-hour days, seven days a week, without pay and without much of a future.

The African Charter and the Convention for the Rights of the Child

A group of local parents from the neighboring community has joined us under the mango tree. We ask them what they think are the rights of children. After pondering for a moment, they answer that we've got the question wrong: parents also have rights, and children have duties as well as rights—it simply seems to make no sense to see the one apart from the other. Having set this matter straight, they explain that children have the right to food and care, and their duty is obedience. Conversely, parents have the right to demand obedience from their children and the duty to feed and care for them. But what about the disobedient children?

Do they try to discipline them? Again there is confusion about the question. No, the parents conclude, disobedient children are left to themselves; rather, the parents invest their time and energy in the "good" kids. Receiving discipline can be a privilege in a society where time for children is scarce and there are so many children to care for and supervise. Even discipline is a tool to help the child develop strength and character, but it must be deserved.

The lesson from this group of parents reminds us of the text of the African Charter on the Rights and Welfare of the Child. Created by the Organization for African Unity (OAU; now called the African Union) in 1989, right after the United Nations created its Convention on the Rights of the Child, the African Charter is on many accounts similar to its UN predecessor, but with one important difference: the first part of the African Charter is named "Rights *and Duties.*" Rights and duties in the relationship between child and parents must have appeared to be so logically intertwined that separating them made no sense. Looking more closely into the preamble of the charter, we find this note: "considering that the promotion and protection of the rights and welfare of the child also implies the performance of duties on the part of everyone."

While the UN convention perceives children's rights as absolute, the African Charter could be interpreted as making them relative, depending on the performance of duties by the child. Children who do not perform according to their duties are not necessarily punished—they may in many cases simply be left to themselves. In practice, this could in fact be perceived as losing their rights to food and care.

In describing child labor, the African Charter (Article 15) is almost a blueprint of the UN convention (Article 32). The only important difference is that the OAU found it necessary to stress that the rights of children to be protected against economic exploitation cover both the formal *and informal* sectors of employment—a clarification probably necessary on a continent where the vast majority of children work in the informal sector. But the African Charter also opens an important window of discretion in the treatment of children. Article 31, on the responsibility of the child, reads:

> Every child shall have responsibilities toward his family and society, the State and other legally recognized communities and the international community. The child, subject to his age and ability, and such limitations as may be contained in the present Charter, shall have the duty: (a) to work for the cohesion of the family, to respect his parents, superiors and elders at all times and to assist them in case of need; (b) to serve his national community by placing his physical and intellectual abilities at its service.

Working for family cohesion? Everyone assists in helping to cover everyday needs like fetching firewood.

The collective rights of the family to unity and welfare thus appear to be more important than the rights and welfare of any one member, including when this member is a child. Presumably, making children work is acceptable as long as the family perceives it to be necessary.

The "right" of the elderly to be able to count on the assistance of any child is furthermore stressed by this paragraph of the charter, and reaffirms the strong element of gerontocracy still present in many African societies. The elderly have long been able to count on their customary claim on children's respect and assistance. There is a strong resistance to challenging this claim, even among many younger Africans who feel they might be denied the reward of the same right when they are old. The situation can be compared to the current protests against public pension reforms in European societies: you pay taxes throughout your active life, and when you retire the younger generation rewards you by paying their taxes, thus ensuring your retirement benefits. In Africa, by serving their own elderly, the young have in fact earned the right to the same reward. In the absence of effective public pension systems, changing this attitude toward the role of the child will therefore be difficult in Africa.

Is Child Labor Intrinsically Bad?

Most of us will agree that children working is not in itself bad. On the contrary, it would probably be harmful if they were never involved in labor. Helping one's parents or making some extra money to fulfill a special wish—it is difficult to imagine a childhood without any work at all. A child who never feels the satisfaction of being useful, or who never gains valued labor skills through practice, is not only a child who misses out on a great deal, but also a child who is poorly prepared for adult life. This may be particularly so in Africa, where harsh realities make work discipline invaluable for everyday survival. Lately, however, with the media spotlight on the most appalling cases of exploitation, the negative sides of child labor have threatened to completely overshadow the positive ones. As a consequence, quickly hatched strategies to combat child labor may risk throwing the baby out with the bath water, and force useful practices underground.

Ever since the UN Convention on the Rights of the Child was ratified in 1989, the international community has been searching for good ways to implement its Article 12, which addresses children's right to be consulted in decisions that are important for their welfare. Children have the right to freely express their views in matters affecting them and also a right to be heard, but when principles meet reality there will inevitably be cases where a child's opinion seems potentially self-destructive in the eyes of an adult. Child rights advocates have run into problems when interviews with child laborers show that many of them in fact *want* to work. Working children in Senegal told researchers that they even saw working as a child right in itself, and that without it they may well lose their very right to survival. Moreover, and somewhat contrary to what had been anticipated, labor and the labor situation were experienced by many children as empowering. Such views give researchers a dilemma: To what extent should we respect working children's expressed desire to work—in particular in situations where survival is not at stake? And what right do we have to argue that their wish to work stems from their limited ability to fully understand their alternatives?

Children's own experience with their work situation is a crucial and

For this 14-year-old girl on the beach at the Togo-Benin border, the workplace is also a social community of women who buy fish and resell them in the market.

often underestimated welfare factor that is obviously more difficult to measure than hours worked and heaviness of tasks. We have constructed two examples that we believe can illustrate how a whole range of perspectives becomes important for assessing the welfare of child laborers. Consider the following two stories.

Little Kemi is a healthy, active 7-year-old girl. She just woke up and is helping her mother prepare the morning meal, which is neither a quick nor an easy task in an African village. She likes preparing breakfast because she will get to nibble before everyone else eats—and she always wakes up ravenous. After breakfast, Kemi's grandmother needs help weeding the kitchen garden. They work side by side, with the older woman telling ghost stories so exciting that before Kemi knows it, lunchtime has arrived. While her mother prepares the meal, Kemi looks after her little sister and has fun tickling and teasing her. After lunch, Kemi plays with some of her friends. At three o'clock most children go back to school, but two girls she likes are going to farm with their father and uncle. Kemi decides to tag along. They sing and joke while they work—the uncle is really funny! He compliments Kemi because she is so helpful and quick. The afternoon flies by and Kemi stays for the evening meal with her friends. She is very satisfied with herself because with a child's understanding, she thinks they could never have done all that work without her help. On her way home from the fields, Kemi brings a bucket of water from the pump, which pleases her mother enormously. Kemi is tired and goes to bed after a full day. She may have worked hard, but she had fun and feels good about herself.

And then there is the flip side of this picture: Johnny is a malnourished 10-year-old boy. He gets up early, even though he is tired and desperately wants to go on sleeping. But he knows if he is late in fixing breakfast for the entire family, Aunt Clarissa may refuse to give him any food. Johnny tries to look busy while they eat, hoping there will be enough left over to satisfy his hunger; there usually is enough, but it's never a sure thing. With longing, Johnny watches the other children in the family go off to school. He really wants to go with them but he has work to do. Although he is cleaning up as fast as he can, Aunt Clarissa berates him for being useless and lazy, and orders him to fetch water at the pump. On the way back home, it is very hot. The long road is dry and the passing vehicles disperse clouds of dust that make Johnny cough. The water is heavy, his head and his back hurt, he feels faint. But Johnny hurries home because nothing is worse than Aunt Clarissa's anger. He no sooner gets home when it is time to turn around and go to the market to sell the food Aunt Clarissa has been cooking. Sales are going well so Johnny decides to take a little rest in the shade. But something terrible happens. While Johnny is sleeping, someone steals his money. Aunt Clarissa is furious. She yells and hits him repeatedly over the head with her fist. Because she does this so often, Johnny almost always has a headache. When Uncle Paul comes home, Aunt Clarissa tells him that the boy has stolen the money, and he beats Johnny too. His cousins watch and laugh before going off to play. As a punishment, Johnny has to skip dinner. He is exhausted and falling asleep is not a problem even on an empty stomach, but he sleeps uneasily and has bad dreams.

Johnny may have worked less than Kemi this day, but no one will hesitate in deciding which child has it better. Neither Kemi nor Johnny has gone to school and both have basically worked all day. Yet Kemi has learned about her ancestors (the grandmother's stories) and about weeding and planting (from her grandmother and her friends' father and uncle), and she is facing life confident of her skills (the uncle's compli-

When a child is malnourished and ill, like this little girl, even the easiest of labor tasks in a safe environment can be harmful.

ments). Johnny, on the other hand, feels useless, scared, and lonely, and he is really hungry. Although his work is not necessarily harmful, his work environment certainly is. In all likelihood, he will develop an aggressiveness that he will sooner or later take out on someone—perhaps his future wife and children. Without education and with few other useful skills for a man, he will not be well suited for the labor market and his ambitions will be low because he has continuously been told how useless he is.

Thirty-five Things That Can Make Child Labor Harmful

We have already mentioned that measurements for child labor tend to be messy. Even combining age and number of hours worked per day, which is about as precise as most datasets can be, gives only a vague indication of the welfare consequences for the working child. Studies of alienation and occupational hazards, for example, make it appear as if the characteristics of the task performed make all the difference. Little attention is generally given to the nature of the tasks performed by children beyond cataloging them by sector. Ideally, we think it would be useful to evaluate child labor from at least three perspectives. The lists below describe characteristics of the tasks performed, the work environment, and most importantly—but sadly most often ignored—the state of the child:

Characteristics of the Tasks

1. Heaviness of work
2. Duration of work
3. Repetitiveness
4. Breaks/rest (conditions of rest)
5. Size and appropriateness of tools/working position
6. Time of day (day or night)
7. Status of work (high status/low status)
8. Degree of freedom in the work situation
9. Rewards (remunerated or not, in cash or kind)
10. Educational value
11. Usefulness of available education lost
12. Responsibility for risky tasks

Characteristics of the Work Environment

13. Colleagues (friends/bullies, adults/children, loneliness)
14. Pollution, chemicals, and dust
15. Hygiene and bacteria

16. Temperature (too hot/too cold)
17. Health hazards (injuries, illnesses)
18. Fears (punishment, food insecurity, threats, wild animals, witchcraft)
19. Psychological climate (scolding or praise)
20. Socialization value
21. Distance to workplace from home (for children living at home)
22. Distance from workplace to family and kin (for children working away from home)

Characteristics of the Child
23. Hours of sleep (in general and previous night)
24. Food intake before, during, and after work
25. Overall nutritional state (current and long-term)
26. Overall health (current and long-term)
27. Overall mental state (willpower, resilience, optimism, capacity to dream)
28. Degree of responsibility (for survival and welfare of family members)
29. Perceived fairness in work situation as compared with siblings and peers
30. Body weight
31. Age/maturity
32. Energy spent on other activities, mainly school and travel
33. Attitude to work (wants to work or not)
34. Number of hours worked that day, that week, that month, and that year
35. Physical effort put into the work (speed and force)

School and Child Labor

It is an oversimplification to assume that schoolchildren don't work and that working children don't go to school. Most African children both work and go to school. Conversely, quite a few African children neither go to school nor work, not because they are spoiled or lazy, but because neither work nor school is realistically accessible for them.

Schooling is commonly assumed to depend on being able to afford it—the richer the parents, the more likely the children will go to school. While this is generally true, African reality is too complex to fit a linear economic model. The linear relationship between schooling and income may hold for better-off African families, but research so far has suggested a different pattern among the great majority of the poor. For poor families, decisions on children's schooling are more likely to be the result of a difficult balancing act that takes into account several factors. The three most immediate questions that parents will have to consider are: What would the children do if they didn't go to school? Who will do the children's work if the children go to school? What will schooling do for the children and for the family?

What Would the Children Do if They Didn't Go to School?

In Mauritania, school enrollment increased remarkably one year following a period of drought. This finding at first baffled researchers because during a drought incomes are likely to drop, making school less affordable. But it made sense considering that the answer to "What would the children do if they didn't go to school?" was "Nothing." Schooling was only perceived to be unaffordable when there were income opportunities for children who stayed out of school. Because children tend to be providers of "adjustable" family labor, going to school depends to a large extent on how much work there is to do at home. If there is work to do on the family farm and the family cannot afford to pay someone to do it, sending a child to school will be expensive. In technical terms, these costs are referred to as alternative or opportunity costs.

The answer to this question thus depends on the demand for child labor, and the demand for child labor in Africa mostly comes from the child's own household. A practical way to determine the child labor demand of poor African households is to look at their possession of productive assets—typically land, tools, and livestock. The more land and livestock, the greater the need for children's help in cultivating the fields and tending the animals. And the more productive these assets are, the more the family loses by not exploiting them fully.[10] This means that the poorest households in poor communities, with little or no assets and property, will sometimes not miss much by sending children to school (the opportunity costs will be low or null). Those with slightly more assets, on the other hand, may need their children's help to make their assets fully productive and therefore will be more likely to keep their children working instead of sending them to school (the opportunity cost of children's schooling will be higher than for the poorest). Finally, those with yet more assets may be able to afford hired help and consequently their children will have a greater chance to be sent to school. Because of this, many studies have found the relationship between household income and school participation to be U-shaped rather than gradually rising. Economist Sonia Bhalotra calls this phenomenon the "wealth paradox" of rural child labor, discussed in more detail later in the chapter.

Who Will Do the Children's Work if the Children Go to School?

When children are sent to school, they often create a (child) labor demand in the household. Who does the work they leave behind? In theory, there are three options: other adults in the household will take over, the children themselves will work harder after school and still do their share, or someone else from outside the household will do it. But where would a poor family find such a person? Children's chores are primarily defined on the basis of their low social status. Thus it may be socially and psychologically difficult for adults to take over these tasks even were they to have the necessary time. Many men would be reluctant to fetch water, for instance, regardless of whether they had the time or strength.

A formally educated population is often more beneficial to society as whole than it is to many of the individual families within it. Introducing compulsory education can therefore be seen as a public taxation of some households, since the adults will suffer not only financially, but also socially and psychologically, if they have to take over children's tasks. The expectation that educated children may bring home more money to the family in the future could perhaps make this sacrifice more bearable, but this expectation will not always be a realistic one. This is often used as the argument for why the public sector needs to invest in schooling: even when the family may not benefit directly from an increased education level, society will. Not surprisingly, the ILO's International Program for the Eradication of Child Labor (IPEC) has estimated that by eradicating child labor and sending all children to school the return to society will be seven dollars to each dollar invested.[11]

So if the children were sent to school, would they be off the hook or not? We found an interesting pattern in our analysis of the Benin UNDP time allocation data, shown in Figure 1.1. Rural children who attend school and rural children who don't have approximately the same number of working hours, schoolwork included: rural girls, both those in school and those not in school, have an average workday of seven and a half hours, while rural boys, both those in school and those not in school, have an average workday of six and a half hours. However, in the urban areas the picture is quite different. Even including schoolwork, children who are in school work much less than the children who are not—on average five hours a day compared to more than eight.[12]

This poster, drawn by a young rural girl for Women in Law and Development in Africa (WILDAF) and Fond Canadien d'Initiatives Locales, speaks for itself.

Figure 1.1   Hours spent working and studying per day in Benin, children 6–14 years old by place of residence, gender, and schooling

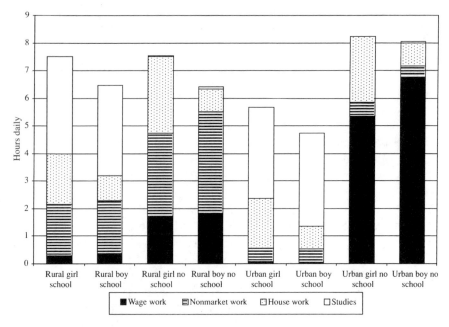

Source: UNDP 1998.

We found one explanation for this difference by examining the background of the children in the sample. In fact, we were able to conclude that many of the non-school-going children working in urban areas are not urban at all. They are the children of poor rural parents who, to a great extent, have been taken into the urban households precisely to fill the child labor gap that was created when the urban children started going to school. We will look more closely at this group of children later in this chapter.

What Will Schooling Do for the Children and for the Family?

It cannot be denied that the schooling offered in some places in Africa is of such poor quality that its usefulness is actually inferior to the education that can be obtained by working with family and friends. This is true when we look at the child's welfare during the learning process as well as in terms of the market value of the skills developed. One would normally think that it is worthwhile to spend time and money studying, because better income later will more than make up for the cost of this education. Most economic models postulate that sending a child to school is an investment in increased future family income, and that this should be an incentive for the parents to send the children to school. While losing child labor income today and even paying school fees and other expenses, a family that invests in the children's education will hope to achieve a much better life later on.

However, this is only an attractive consideration for a family that has the necessary means to survive while covering such investments. The very poor typically lack the means to make investments of almost any kind, and moreover, when they face the various small crises that so frequently hit poor families in Africa, they simply have no reserves. As a result they are forced to exploit any resource available—including their children. Access to short-term credit could perhaps help poor families get through temporary problems without taking the children out of school, but reliable credit is scarce in most rural areas. Access to low-interest long-term education loans, which could help cover schooling expenses in the first place, is even more rare.

But again, few relationships are clear and predictable in Africa, and this also applies to the relationship between children's schooling and future income. For example, researchers we interviewed in Burkina Faso insisted that there was actually a negative economic return to formal schooling in rural areas. This was explained by the high unemployment of educated people, who could not find jobs corresponding to their expectations and often refused manual labor for which they felt overqualified. Rural youth in West Africa who had learned French migrated to unemployment (and in some cases to prostitution and crime) in the city. At the end of the day, they were worse off than their less-educated peers who had remained in the village. Similarly, a study in Ethiopia found that formal education only made a difference for people lucky enough to find a job in the formal sector, while for work in the informal sector (which employs the vast majority of people in Africa), returns from education were basically zero, and the only significant determinant of wages was the entrepreneur's level of capital.[13]

The weakening of social capital in many African societies has also affected the traditional bonds of mutuality within families. It is no wonder that rural parents fear that their educated children will migrate and be gone forever—and with them the parents' investment in their schooling, not to mention their old-age insurance. From a rational perspective, there are good reasons why some parents will choose to profit from the labor of their children while they are still controllable. This affects girls in particular, since their future earnings (and labor) tend to belong to their future husband and his family.

Poverty and Child Labor

Assuming that parents will do everything they can to give their children a bright future, it is common to believe that child labor is a last resort for poor families. On the other hand, as previously indicated, concern for an individual child in Africa cannot be at variance from overall family concerns. We have also pointed out how child labor may be seen to build character, and therefore may be desirable. Both these observations make the theoretical assumption of the altruistic parent more complicated. This may help to explain why the relationship between child labor and poverty is far from clear in Africa. Some researchers have found no relationship at all, while those working on data from rural areas have found the opposite of what they expected—slightly richer children working more than do the poorest children. An example from a study finding no significant relationship between wealth level (measured in expenditure per capita) and child labor participation is shown in Figure 1.2. While wealth clearly increases the probability of schooling, it shows no similar effect on child labor participation in this case. It is also worth noticing that the wealth increase shown in the graph is enormous: even by quadrupling real expenditure per capita, no effect can be seen on child labor participation. To complicate things further, in the cases where researchers did find the expected impact of poverty on child labor, the effect was often marginal.[14]

Yet we know from more global studies from other parts of the world

Figure 1.2   Probability of going to school and of working in rural areas by welfare levels

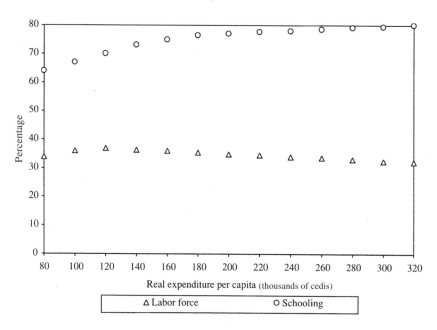

Source: Canagarajah and Coulombe 1997.

that, in general, the poorer a family is, the more likely its children are to work. So why should Africa be different? Part of the answer can be found by looking at global trends. It is true that poorer countries tend to have higher rates of child labor, but there does not appear to be a linear relationship. Below a certain level of poverty, child labor rates stop increasing systematically regardless of how low incomes go. Most African countries are below this level altogether, meaning that the effect of marginal changes in poverty on child labor seems to be overridden by the effect of other factors. As Figure 1.3 shows, African countries with widely different gross domestic product (GDP) per capita have about the same child labor rates, and countries with the same GDP per capita have widely different child labor rates. Researchers asking similar questions have also found similar tendencies. For example, a study examining the effect of credit access on child labor had to remove the sub-Saharan African countries from the analysis in order to obtain significant results at a global level.[15]

Economist Sonia Bhalotra describes the often counterintuitive relationship between poverty and child labor in rural Africa as a "wealth

Figure 1.3   Child labor rate and GDP per capita for selected African countries

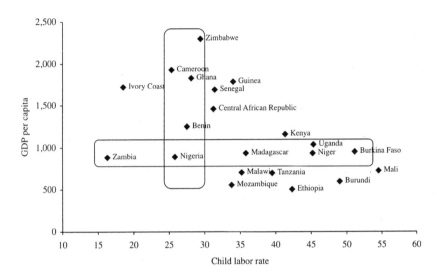

Source: Andvig, Canagarajah, and Kielland 2001.
Note: Three atypical African countries—South Africa, Botswana, and Gabon, which have substantially higher incomes—have not been included in order to clarify our point.

paradox." With data from Ghana, she shows how the child labor participation rate increases with the size of farmland owned by the child's family. The same is the case at the community level: child labor opportunities on farmland owned by others in the community increase child labor participation, even for children of landless households. Not only does the time spent on farm work increase, but so does the time spent working in general, probably because of substitution effects between parental farm work and domestic work.[16]

Ownership of land and land availability in the community are probably important keys to understanding the wealth paradox. Because income and consumption are hard to measure in rural areas, it is common to use "wealth," determined primarily by livestock, assets, and land possessions, as a proxy for poverty. The problem is that this measurement of wealth also measures something completely different, namely the *opportunity cost* of schooling. The cost of sending a child to school is higher if the family could have used the child's labor to increase the productivity of its farmland than if there were no productive work for the child to do in the first place. When the variable "wealth" has two potentially opposite effects on child labor, researchers often end up with puzzling results. And since the share of poor people who live on smaller farms is so much higher in Africa than on other continents, the wealth paradox has naturally also appeared as much more of an African research problem.

There is also another interesting twist to the wealth paradox. Several authors have pointed out that credit constraints can contribute to an increase in child labor.[17] Bhalotra, however, points out that when there is limited access to credit in a society, collateral matters, regarding both access to the credit as well as the interest rate one can negotiate (the same pattern is found by another researcher in Côte d'Ivoire, as shown in Figure 1.4). If children work more when the family has a larger farm, this could be counteracted by the fact that the families with larger farms would have better access to the limited credit available compared to families with smaller farms and less child labor.[18]

Carol Ann Rogers and Kenneth A. Swinnerton bring up another interesting economic argument.[19] Economic literature maintains that an important motivation for parents to send their children to school is the expectation that educated children will be able to provide better for their needs in old age. Rogers and Swinnerton observe that the better off the parents are, the less likely the children are to contribute when the parents

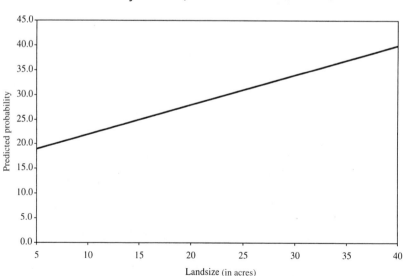

Figure 1.4   Predicted probability of working in rural areas by land size, evidence from Côte d'Ivoire

Source: Coulombe 1998.

grow old. Within a sample of relatively poor families—as we typically find in Africa—we may therefore see that small income improvements for the parents could reduce their expectations of future support from their children, something that will also reduce their incentive to send children to school. If we see the parents' investment in their children's education as a loan that will be paid back with the children's future contributions, this loan becomes more expensive the less likely the children are to give back to their parents. One could furthermore assume that less-than-destitute parents also *depend* less on the future support of their children, and therefore see less of a reason to invest in it.

Another way to illustrate the complex relationship between wealth and child labor is to add cultural considerations to the equation. Take the example of the Peuhl of West Africa. They are mostly cattle-raising people, and the value of their cattle is often high. However, while the value of their cattle makes them wealthy compared to the farmers in the same area, cattle are also labor-intensive. Since herding is a task commonly assigned to children, the "wealthy" Peuhl will be more likely than their farming neighbors to have their children working (the wealth paradox). But the issue is even more complex. Should the family need cash for the hospitalization of a sick child, obtaining it by selling a cow would be nearly unthinkable and would generally be perceived as a much more drastic coping strategy than sending another child to work for a wage. It would be difficult even to compare the two. Because the children belong to the women's sphere and the cattle to the men's, it is hardly imaginable that one should convert a value within one sphere into support for a need belonging to the other. Cattle are the backbone of the Peuhl life and economy in general: slaughtering a milk cow will bring long-term thirst to the entire family.

Whether a child will work or not depends at least in part on social and cultural considerations that are not necessarily related to economic factors and that are not a mere function of the total labor demand in the household. The status of certain tasks matters greatly. As hierarchies are defined by gender, position, and age, it is normally clear who will do what when a group of people are together. In some places, carrying is perceived as a low-status task. Typically one will see that the woman carries when she is with a man, but when children are present, they will share the burden. Should the children be unavailable to do the carrying because they are in school, their father may suffer a status loss by having to do it himself. The impact of this status loss will depend on the importance assigned to such status values by the family and the overall community and how they compare to the prestige obtained by sending children to school.

Ruralization and Child Labor

While poverty seems to have several different effects on child labor rates within sub-Saharan Africa, Figure 1.5 shows that ruralization and child labor seem to be much more clearly related. Alongside the low availability of schooling in many rural areas, the main reason is probably that the survival of rural families depends heavily on subsistence farming, and survival needs generally produce a labor demand that is not very flexible.

Moreover, farm work is relatively well suited for children, since most of it requires moderate skills and little supervision, and household income in farming communities is often restricted primarily by limitations in the available work force. When the effect of farm work becomes so powerful that it confounds statistical work on poverty and child labor,

Children are often in charge of carrying water, like this little girl in Burkina Faso.

Figure 1.5   Child labor rate and ruralization for selected African countries

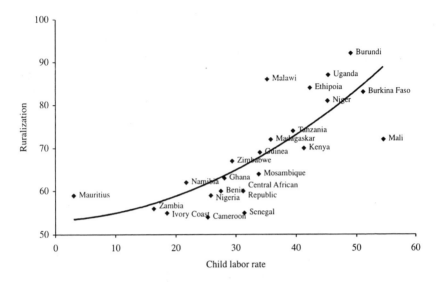

Source: World Bank's World Development Indicators.

this is mainly due to the fact that the overwhelming majority of child labor takes place within farming. For example, in a study on Zambia it is argued that 80 percent of child labor takes places in subsistence agriculture,[20] and a time allocation study in northern Sudan finds that 88 percent of child labor is in agriculture.[21]

Distance, lack of transportation, and low mechanization often combine to make rural life extremely labor intensive. Everyone is expected to contribute, children included, because tasks that take little or no time in an urban setting—like getting a glass of water—become extremely time consuming where basic infrastructure and services are missing. In the village, food is obtained the slow way, by planting, weeding, harvesting, transporting, processing, and cooking. The endlessly repeated scenes of women and children pounding yams or cassava, piling seeds, and drying foods, strike most foreigners who travel through the African countryside. Foreigners are also likely to remember the endless rows of women and children carrying wood, water, and agricultural products to their homes or the nearest market, often a several-hour walk away, and often in very high temperatures.

The hard work, high burden of disease, and lack of education turn rural life into a routine of day to day survival and labor into a virtue. Work methods are learned at an early age and repeated throughout a lifetime. It is easily understandable that the capacity to "think new" and be creative about how best to organize and reform labor practices becomes very limited under such difficult conditions. Rural areas consequently tend to be more traditional, and we can only assume that the rural poor find a certain comfort in routines and in traditional work forms. So-called development interventions tend to interrupt fragile equilibria, and we should not be amazed to find hostility toward new norms and modern inventions. The restructuring demanded by changing child-rearing patterns and sending children to school will often cause a dramatic breach with the safe routines and upset both family and community life.

Women and Child Labor

Children in Africa tend to belong to the women's sphere, and in particular the younger children spend most of their time with their mothers. Women are the principal employers of the youngest child labor in Africa, as well as of older girls.[22] In her anthropological work on child labor in rural Zimbabwe, Pamela Reynolds suggested that

> girls work harder than boys because women direct children's labor and are able to control girls more firmly . . . but there is more than that. The ethos of womanliness is "the dull compulsion" of daily work. Girls are reluctant apprentices. A woman's duty is to bind her daughter into service in order to secure her future as a farmer and a useful servant in the kinship network.[23]

Most research shows that the tasks performed by young children, in particular, tend to be typical women's tasks—carrying, subsistence agriculture, and housework. Boys will sometimes do men's work if there are not enough men around to perform such tasks. On the other hand, boys will also perform women's tasks when they are with other men, and typically take on the labor role of women in men's workplaces. As an example, child soldiers will often be expected to do laundry, cook, and carry for the adult combatants. In an article titled "Women's Power, Children's Labor," Candice Bradley summarizes four main reasons why children do women's work more often than men's work:[24]

1. Girls and younger boys tend to gravitate to the same physical space as women, so they are assigned tasks by women in a women's environment.
2. Work occupies children and keeps them out of their mothers' way.

3. Children's work may increase their mothers' productivity if children substitute for women in low-return, open-access tasks.
4. Boys sometimes take the place of women in men's work groups (e.g., by bringing water or cooking).

It is hard to ignore the fact that the rank order in most African societies is maintained in a rather authoritarian way. Women are mostly seen as ranking lower than men and are sometimes fully under their husband's, father's, or brother's administration. The elderly are typically at the top of the status list, followed by men, boys above a certain age, women, and then girls and small children.

As shown in Table 1.1, women's workdays are generally longer than

This widow (resting in the tent) ran away from forced marriage to her late husband's brother. She now lives in a quarry where she and her children crack and transport rocks for a living. It is common to assume overlapping interests of women and children. However, women are the main employers of African children.

Table 1.1 Differences in men's and women's workdays in selected African time allocation studies

	Female	Male	Difference
Benin	9.9	8.0	1.9
Botswana (1984)	10.3	8.8	1.5
Botswana (1994)	6.2	5.1	1.1
Burkina Faso	14.3	8.7	5.6
Central African Republic	7.0	5.2	1.8
Côte d'Ivoire	7.0	4.3	2.7
Kenya	12.3	8.1	4.2
Nigeria	14.0	8.5	5.5
Tanzania	9.5	7.6	1.9
Zambia	12.2	7.2	5.0

Sources: Brown and Haddad 1994, Mueller 1984, and UNDP 1998.

men's. Moreover, Eva Mueller found that adult men in rural Botswana work 25 percent less than women and actually less than most children, having about the same amount of leisure time as 7- to 9-year-old boys).[25] The status of the tasks, in combination with the status of the individuals available to perform them, will decide who does what.

In some urban societies, most notably in conservative Muslim areas, women are expected not to leave the household at all. However, with the help of their children for transport and errands, they still often run a business out of their home. Loretta Bass describes this availability of child labor to Hausa women in northern Nigeria as an institution that at first glance seems to strengthen the position and bargaining power of women within the household. This dependency produces a general reluctance to sending children to school, because of the short-term costs the lost child labor would mean to women. However, Mueller points out another and more long-term implication of the practice: letting children facilitate and enable women's economic activities under the purdah system (seclusion of women from public observation) is in fact helping to institutionalize and thereby secure the maintenance of a practice that on a larger scale deprives women of rights and influence and that might not have been able to survive without the use of child labor.[26]

While the oppression of African women has been given considerable attention, the fact that women tend to delegate work to the next level down the social hierarchy—that is, to their children (and in particular to their foster children)—has been much less researched and written about. Pamela Reynolds calls for a more systematic investigation of child labor, and writes that this is necessary because child labor is vital to women. The burden of running a household, farming and feeding a family has increased for many of Africa's women. Men's labor is often denied them because of migrant work or because they concentrate on cash farming, and children's labor is curtailed because of school. The toll on women's physical energy and their isolation has not been adequately measured.[27]

Knowing the hardship of African women, it is easy to argue that they need protection and understanding. It is important to realize, however, that hardship also can produce cynicism, aggression, and sometimes selfishness, and that these feelings may be taken out on those even more powerless—the children.[28] Interviewing maltreated working children, we have been struck by one common feature: the perpetrator in most cases was a woman, either directly or indirectly by encouraging her husband or other men to punish the child. We know little about the mental health of African women and of issues like alcoholism and drug abuse, as the research literature on these topics is very limited. However, several maltreated child domestic servants told us that their mistress employer was drinking when she was home alone with them and that drinking made her violent. While these children were not always aware of what alcoholism is, they did recall that their mistress's husband accused her of being a drunk, or that she drank from bottles that gave off a strong smell. Odile, who is pictured in Chapter 6, had her hands broken because she bought the wrong brand of beer for her mistress.

Both governments and donors commonly run children's programs through women and notably through mothers. While it is correct that mothers tend to be the primary caretaker of children, and the parent most likely to cover their expenses for food, health,[29] and schooling,[30] it is important to remember that the interests of women and children don't always overlap. On the contrary, the interests of children may even be in conflict with those of their mothers. As mentioned previously, compulsory primary school could be perceived as a public taxation of the household economy. Making children go to school is indeed more specifically a taxation of the woman, who will often have to pay the school fees for the child, and will in addition be burdened with traditional child tasks while the children are in school. This will not only degrade her socially, but may even force her away from the commercial labor market because she will have to spend much more of her time on household chores that would normally be left to children. Needless to say, without her own source of income, her bargaining power, independence, and status will decline even further. The reverse is also true: time-consuming training programs for women may increase the labor burden on their children and sometimes even threaten their children's chances of going to school. In Niger it was similarly documented that child labor increased when women were helped to start up income-generating activities.[31]

Foster Care and Child Labor

"Since you are so concerned with child fostering, why don't you interview me and my colleagues?" jokes the principal of an African management-training institute. He picks a mango that is hanging just above his head, slices it open with his pocketknife, and offers it to us. He continues: "Even *we* were all 'placed' children at one point or another." Indeed, sending children to live in an informal foster care arrangement with other extended family members—commonly referred to as child placement —is neither new nor rare.[32] It is thanks to this kind of support from family and friends that many of today's government officials, professionals, and teachers in Africa received the education that enabled them to attain their present positions. And it is thanks to the fostering tradition that Africans have been able to take care of AIDS orphans to the best of their ability, and that the street child problem is still fairly limited.

While recent attention has been given to discrimination against foster children, a range of different fostering arrangements of very different value are actually practiced. In a classic paper, Uche Isiugo-Abanihe sorts African fostering arrangements into five main categories: kinship fostering, crisis fostering, alliance and apprentice fostering, domestic fostering, and educational fostering.[33] Our friend the principal and his colleagues mainly fall into the last of these categories. Mamane Bozari lists as many as nine types of child placement in a study from Niger, ranging from full adoption to desperate submission into slaverylike social contracts.[34]

Based on available figures from twenty-six countries, around 14 percent of African children age 14 and under live away from both their mother and their father. Namibia and South Africa have the highest figures, with 29 and 25 percent respectively. For the great majority of these children, 73 percent, both parents are alive.[35]

Although originally a well-intended and most valuable institution, there is evidence that African child placement systems increasingly conceal the exploitation of "in-fostered" child labor. As mentioned earlier, it appears that poor rural children are being sent to town to do the work that urban children who go to school no longer do. Additionally, they are increasingly assigned the domestic chores that women employed in the formal sector no longer have time for nor want. Richer families will be able to afford "real" servants, but many will have to rely on someone cheaper—a child.

Although "placed children" constitute an internally diverse group, they generally have lower school participation rates than do their peers across the continent.[36] Interestingly, it has also been found that in several countries school participation rates are higher than normal among regular children who live in a household where an orphan has been placed. This indicates that the work contribution of the placed child in fact enables the household to free up its own children and send them to school.[37] The welfare consequences of this development are brutal. Side by side in the same household are first-class children who play and go to school, and second-class children who work all day with no time for education or leisure.

Why would a household want to send its child to live with someone else? Each case can be seen as the result of the combination of demand (or "pull") factors in the receiving household, and supply (or "push") factors in the child's parental home.[38] And each decision is the result of several considerations under which the interest of the child may or may not be given weight.

First, the primary concern may be to give *the child* the opportunity for a better life, for instance by sending him or her to live closer to a school. This is often the case for bright kids who did well in the primary grades and need to move to a place near a secondary school. Needless to say, this kind of child placement is more common for boys than for girls. Sometimes the children of migrants are sent back to their country or area of origin in order to be raised in a safe environment, or to learn about their family's culture.[39] Children can also be placed in an apprenticeship with an artisan, or simply to allow them to live in more prosperous areas, be around educated people, and hopefully develop better social skills in their presence. Not surprisingly, the latter is more often the case for girls, and the hope that they will be able to find a relatively well-off husband is, in many cases, an important motivator.

Second, we may find that the primary concern is to help *the child's parents*. Typical cases are when a child is sent away to make it possible for one of the parents to remarry or migrate, or to obtain goodwill from the host family. In other places the labor contribution of a placed child is reimbursed by a monthly sum to the child's parents, but even when it is not, it may be to the parents' advantage to have one less mouth to feed.

Third, *the receiving household* may be the main beneficiary, as in the case of child domestic servitude. Children are also typically moved to keep elderly members company, to enhance the lives of childless couples, or to provide services typical of a child of a given sex to families that only have working-age children of the opposite sex.[40] Finally, child placement may be undertaken primarily to benefit *family kinship.* Where child labor is common, the family may choose to move children away from nonproductive areas and into other parts of the family where there is a labor demand. The family as a whole will benefit if the child's labor capacity is used where it gives the highest return. Family kinship may also benefit socially from moving children around, as this strengthens the mutual interdependency of the family. It should to be stressed that the receiving household often has not asked for the foster child in the first place; the decision of the child placement has been made by family elders or by a family council, and the household in question is simply not given an opportunity to protest. Understanding this also helps us understand why many households do not seem to feel very responsible for the welfare of their foster children.

In all of these cases it becomes important to find out how badly the family needs to send the child away—that is, how good the alternatives or how big the losses will be if they don't. There is a clear difference between wanting to send a child away to go to a slightly better school, and wanting to send a child away to save him or her from hunger, even though both acts may be in the child's best interests. Parents may want to send a child away to improve their own living standard, but they may also be forced to do so in order to be able to feed younger siblings. Similarly, a childless couple may want to have a child for social reasons, while an elderly relative may be unable to survive alone.

At the receiving end, we can assume that most decisions to take in a child are based on a combination of economic and social motives. On the one hand a receiving family may seek free and docile labor, while on the other it may feel responsible for helping the child to live a better life, or for helping the parents through a hardship—having very little choice but to help out while a relative is ill or in jail, for example. Again, which motive dominates will make a big difference to the child. A receiving family may argue, or even convince itself, that its main motive is helping out poor rural relatives by raising their child, while the real motive may be that the family needs someone to carry out low-status tasks in the household—and what better help than a child who will not even ask to be paid?

The welfare prospects of the child depend on the reasons that dominated the "placement" decision on the sending and receiving sides. A child who has to leave the parental household in a crisis runs a higher risk of economic exploitation, because his or her parents are not in a position to negotiate the placement conditions. Similarly, a child who is "invited" into a foster family predominantly for economic reasons runs a greater risk of being exploited and emotionally neglected than does a child who is wanted to fulfill the lives of a childless couple. There is reason to believe that placed children are at higher risk today than in earlier times. The monetarization of many child placement arrangements plays an important role in this picture. In one area we visited, people could even give a date for when parents had started to ask for monthly fees from their children's host families: it had happened after a drought. A household that pays a monthly sum for a child will clearly look upon him or her with different eyes, and expect something in return.

With the introduction of formal schooling, the gap in life quality and future prospects between school-going and non-school-going children deepened. Not surprisingly, there is a systematic link between school attendance and the child's biological relationship to the head-of-household, particularly for girls. The closer the child's family ties to the head-of-household, the more likely he or she is to go to school. In Burkina Faso, for example, school attendance rates for urban girls are 74 percent if they live in their father's household, 47 percent if they live with a close relative, 39 percent if they live with a more remote relative, and only 19 percent if they live in the household of someone to whom they are not related.[41] A study reviewing school attendance for orphans throughout Africa produced similar results: their attendance varies with the degree of relatedness between themselves and their adult caregivers.[42] Time allocation data provide further evidence to confirm this tendency. In Benin, children who don't live with their parents work an average of eighty minutes more per day than those who do.[43] In particular, girls living with an urban family to whom they are not related work an average of three hours more than their peers. In fact, a girl "placed" in an urban family in Benin works an average of seventy-five hours per week.[44]

In some countries, child placement in a nonrelated household is increasingly brokered by an intermediary who often benefits from the matchmaking between sending and receiving families. This tends to blur the difference between brokered child placement and another scary practice: the development of organized child trafficking.

Trafficking and Child Labor

The official definition of trafficking is drawn from the so-called Palermo Protocol[45] to the UN Convention Against Transnational Organized Crime. Its Article 3 reads:

(a) "Trafficking in persons" shall mean the recruitment, transportation, transfer, harbouring or receipt of persons, by means of the threat
or use of force or other forms of coercion, of abduction, of fraud, of
deception, of the abuse of power or of a position of vulnerability or of
the giving or receiving of payments or benefits to achieve the consent
of a person having control over another person, for the purpose of
exploitation. Exploitation shall include, at a minimum, the exploitation or the prostitution of others or other forms of sexual exploitation,
forced labour or services, slavery or practices similar to slavery,
servitude or the removal of organs; (b) The consent of a victim of
trafficking in persons to the intended exploitation set forth in subparagraph (a) of this article shall be irrelevant where any of the means set
forth in subparagraph (a) have been used; (c) The recruitment, transportation, transfer, harbouring or receipt of a child for the purpose of
exploitation shall be considered "trafficking in persons" even if this
does not involve any of the means set forth in subparagraph (a) of this
article; (d) "Child" shall mean any person under eighteen years of
age.

International conventions and global definitions are challenged by a
myriad of local scenarios within which they are supposed to be applied.
Labor migration, nomadic cultures, general wanderlust, and various
child-fostering practices are so commonplace in Africa that it is often
difficult to see any clear distinction between what is tradition and what
has recently been labeled as aberrant and criminal.[46] Consequently, the
way "trafficking" has been defined and debated has provoked many
Africans who feel that international actors are criminalizing a behavior
that older generations still perceive to be beneficial to the child and to
society. Although trafficking can refer to both in-country and cross-border transfers of children, this chapter focuses mainly on the cross-border
cases. With some exceptions, international trafficking takes the children
farther away from their family, kin, ethnic group, and language community. It is also considered an international crime that leaves the child
without a legal status in his or her new country.

In 2000, West African governments met with the International
Labour Organization (ILO) and the United Nations Children's Fund
(UNICEF) in Libreville, Gabon, to discuss the child-trafficking situation. A regional definition of child trafficking was developed during the
conference. It was designed with the explicit purpose of clarifying the
differences between children who were "exported" to exploit their labor
and children who were in fact "placed" in accordance with regional traditional practices, similar to what has been described previously. The
definition reads: "For the transfer of children to qualify as trafficking,
there should be: 1. the conclusion of a transaction;[47] 2. the intervention
of an intermediary; 3. the motive to exploit."

While there is every reason to be culturally sensitive, cultural sensitivity can be overdone, with the result that traditional behaviors that may be harmful end up becoming protected or at least condoned.[48] In this case, the West African definition uses the existence of a demonstrable economic motive and of an intermediary as the core distinction between *traditional* child placement and *criminal* child trafficking. It thus ignores the obvious economic motives behind traditional child placement as well as the fact that direct arrangements between parents and employers (made without the use of intermediaries) can be highly exploitative of children. The absence of a more explicit definition of the term *exploitation* may in fact contribute to blurring, rather than to facilitating, identification of the "real" victims of child trafficking.

In a market in a small village, a mother offered our assistant Martine her 10-year-old girl, who is being interviewed in this picture. We asked if she wanted to go with us to the capital. She answered yes, without hesitation.

*   *   *

In 2001 the child-trafficking situation in West Africa hit the headlines of the international media.[49] When the ship *Etireno* was reported lost off the coast of Cameroon, rumors spread that there were as many as 200 child slaves on board. When the ship returned to the port of Cotonou two weeks later, only 42 children were found. But the *Etireno* was no special case. The organized migration of children and adults directed toward wealthy Gabon had been under way for many years, and many a ship has sailed the same route as the *Etireno*. According to a more precise definition of slavery (provided later in this chapter), hardly any of the children aboard strictly qualified as potential slaves, nor as victims of trafficking. The nongovernmental organization (NGO) Terre des Hommes, which received the *Etireno* children, reported that in only a few cases had there been any transfer of money. According to the NGO Anti-Slavery International, children trafficked to Gabon can in most cases expect to be paid a salary when they arrive there. The salary for a child domestic worker in Gabon, according to Anti-Slavery International, is often equivalent to the salary of a public employee in a country like Togo, something that makes the phenomenon resemble adult economic migration. The main difference, however, is that children have much weaker negotiating power, leaving them with few options but to stay and work, regardless of how exploitative their employers are. The previously mentioned problem of first-class versus second-class children becomes even more explicit in a country like Gabon, where most local children go to school while the imported children work, and where ethnic differences strongly limit mobility between the two groups.

Before child trafficking hit the spotlight, the Beninese government bravely and openly admitted the problem, which was at the time an issue of denial and rejection in many neighboring countries. A massive household survey concluded that in 2000 there were as many as 50,000 Beninese children 6–16 years old working away from their families outside the national borders,[50] constituting as much as 4 percent of the rural child population. The boys had left mainly for Côte d'Ivoire, where commercial agriculture is labor-demanding, while the majority of girls left to become domestic servants in Gabon. A similar survey in Burkina Faso two years later found that as many as 83,000 Burkinabe children were working abroad, and that 66,000 of them were working in Côte d'Ivoire.[51] Extrapolating from the Benin and the Burkina Faso findings, we estimate that some 250,000 West Africa children currently work outside their own countries.[52]

But were the children reported as working outside their countries in the two studies indeed victims of trafficking? Or was this rather related to opportunity seeking? Or was it, as Sarah Castle and Aisse Diarra suggest in a study from Mali, a rite of passage?[53] The Benin study led to an astonishing finding—the transborder child labor migration observed was not necessarily the result of poverty. In fact, when village households were divided into quintiles according to their wealth, it turned out that the poorest households were not the ones most likely to send their children away to work (see Figure 1.6).[54] Also in the Burkina Faso study, the link to poverty was weak, and in fact it was significant only in the case of internal trafficking of girls. As a further complication to using poverty as a main explanatory factor, it was found that local access to formal credit systematically increased instead of reducing the child labor migration.

An explanation for this came from a farmer in a village identified as a high supplier of "exported" children: "You see, if you don't have a child in Côte d'Ivoire, you don't count in this village," he told us. "You are not consulted." What we had initially thought was motivated by economic need, or even despair, was in fact a status symbol in his village. Not all families had the capacity to organize their children's labor migration. It took a large social network, a certain level of organization, and money to initiate the travel. This is why it was not the poorest but the slightly better-off households that had sent the most children abroad.

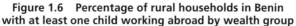

Figure 1.6   Percentage of rural households in Benin with at least one child working abroad by wealth group

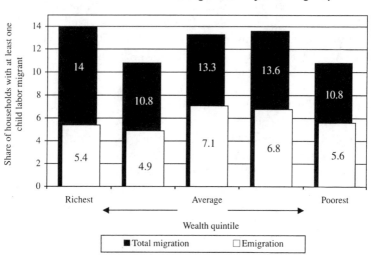

Source: Benin child migration data.

As it turned out, the case where the trafficker shows up at the village to recruit children was perhaps the best known, but certainly not the most common. Instead, most of the children came to depend on more or less well-meaning "helpers" during the journey. Some were recruited by intermediaries at car stations and border stations on their way.

* * *

When child trafficking is discussed, children tend to be treated as passive victims of adult decisionmaking. But we have found that children themselves often influence the decision to go abroad.[55] The *Washington Post* printed a story from Mali that illustrates this: A boy saw a young man wearing a pair of spotless Nikes, and couldn't avoid noticing how cool he looked compared to all the other men in the village wearing flip-flops. He heard that the young man had been to Côte d'Ivoire. The next morning the boy got up early and walked for many miles until he reached a town. In the car station, he met a man who said he could help him get to Côte d'Ivoire. The man was a professional trafficker and what happened next is no surprise. The boy returned home one year later, after months of torment on a coffee farm. Probably desperate to save face, he spent the little money he had earned on a pair of Nikes. He did not tell anyone in the village what he had been through. But the other kids probably noticed the Nikes and heard that he went to Côte d'Ivoire.[56] The story is echoed in the report from Castle and Diarra, who indeed found that children not only had their personal motives for leaving, but also in many cases initiated the migration against the will of their parents. It is no coincidence that, according to UNICEF, most children intercepted during a process of trafficking report being annoyed, because in fact they are eager to go.[57]

Sexual Trafficking and Child Labor

The greatest difference between the use of children for common labor tasks and the use of children for commercial sexual exploitation is the enormous potential for profit in the latter case. High profits enable relatively sophisticated crime syndicates to develop advanced trafficking routes, and buy the complicity of police and customs officials. In addition to the syndicates, unscrupulous individuals also take advantage of children in difficult situations like war and natural disaster, often after they have become separated from their parents during migration, flight, and refuge. The trafficker typically promises to help, but at the end of the trip the child is forced into prostitution. While occasional trading of sex for fees and services sometimes occurs among urban youth in many African countries, the victims of sex trafficking are terrorized psychologically and physically so they will continue to accept abuse. Furthermore, they rarely get much of the income from their sexual exploitation. The children in question are often held captive and closely watched, with few or no opportunities to escape. In fact, it must be questioned if this type of exploitation of children can be considered as "labor" in the first place. Extreme child abuse and sexual assault may be a better description.

In the case of child trafficking for more common tasks, both parents and traffickers can to a certain degree justify their acts by saying that it is in the interest of the child to leave the hard work and poor prospects of subsistence agriculture for wage labor in more developed areas or countries. But the obvious misery and horrible prospects of the victims of child prostitution leave no room for such justifications. While trafficking for agricultural or domestic work in many cases may resemble traditional fostering arrangements, child trafficking for sexual exploitation resembles slavery. The people involved are consequently of a much more cynical nature and are often involved in other criminal activities.

South Africa is perhaps the country where the trafficking of children for commercial sexual exploitation has been best documented, although the phenomenon is also common in East Africa and in Nigeria. Like other relatively wealthier countries in Africa, South Africa is a prominent target for trafficking, with numerous victims coming from within the country as well as from other countries in the region, notably Angola and Mozambique but also Zambia, Senegal, Kenya, Tanzania, Uganda, and Ethiopia. It is reported that children may be as young as seven, and that many of them are victims of debt bondage.[58] South Africa is also believed to be a transition country for African girls on their way to other destinations, such as Bangkok. Interestingly, a Thai report claims that South Africa is also a primary destination for Thai child prostitutes.[59]

Another country infamous for trafficking women and girls into prostitution is Nigeria, which is a provider of prostitutes to most of its neighboring countries but also to Italy and Belgium. Italian police have registered 10,000 Nigerian prostitutes in Italy, many of them underage, but NGOs working with them estimate the real number to be at least double this amount.[60] The mafia running the organized trafficking of Nigerian prostitutes is extremely sophisticated. For a fee of $50,000 a girl can be taken to Europe, where she will work as a prostitute until the debt is paid (board and lodging will also have to be paid). The route to Europe goes through several African countries and travel papers are replaced several times on the way. In the destination country, the girl is obliged to pay regular installments to a "mama" (e.g., a minimum of $100 a day). Because of threats of violence against herself and her family in Nigeria, she is left with little choice but to comply. However, trafficking from Nigeria also has a cultural dimension that is perhaps even more binding. Before departure, the girl and her family are taken to the local shrine, where traditional animist religious leaders bless the pact and the girl is sworn to silence and compliance. In other cases, the vodun ceremony may take place during the trip or even at the destination.

"They took a lock of my hair, my menstrual blood, pubic hair, and even my panties and bra," explained Esohe, a Nigerian teenager rescued from prostitution in Italy, "and they burned them. They told me that if I didn't do what they told me, I will go mad." So the fear of a supernatural punishment keeps the payments coming and ensures no attempts to escape. This could be the reason why Italian police so far have had little success in obtaining names of traffickers from detained Nigerian girls.

Prostitutes are normally deported from Italy after being caught for the third time. It is striking, however, that most deportees claim that they were deported just about the time when they had completed the payment of their debt and were ready to start working for themselves. It is not unreasonable to hypothesize that someone deliberately reports them to the police in order to sweep the streets of independent competition, or that corrupt police officers are no longer "motivated" to turn a blind eye once a girl is free of her pimp.

Slavery and Child Labor

Slavery is generally seen as a thing of the past. Only Sudan and Mauritania are still recognized as having slavery in its traditional sense, understood as people being sold, bought, and "legally" owned. In both countries, racial and religious characteristics are important in defining the difference between the slaves and the masters, and in both cases there are Arabized Muslim owners of black Christian or animist slaves. Children are bought or born into slavery, and underage girls are taken as "wives" of their master and give birth to his children. Beyond this traditional type of slavery, children's labor situations are sometimes so strikingly unfair and exploitative that it does not seem like an exaggeration to call them slavery. Yet accusing a person or a country of child slavery is extremely serious and so insulting that a clear and preferably conservative definition is needed.

In his book *Disposable People: New Slavery in the Global Economy,* sociologist Kevin Bales provides some criteria that can be used to avoid confusion as to what constitutes slavery in modern times.[61] In traditional slavery, there was a very large distance between the place of origin of people seen as "enslavable" and the labor-intensive production areas where they were to be used. Consequently, it was extremely expensive to transport the slaves to their destination—most commonly from Africa to the Caribbean, Brazil, and the United States. The price of slaves could thus become very high and the annual return on their labor was often as low as 5 percent of their original price. These economic realities could make it necessary to have the slaves work for fifteen to twenty years in order to recoup the initial investment. This in turn had two consequences. First, legal ownership was required in order to ensure profitability. Second, the slaves needed to be "maintained" to a reasonable degree to keep them productive over such a long time. A slave owner could perhaps afford to kill one slave to set an example to the others and thereby increase their productivity. However, only a stupid owner would kill or otherwise hurt his slaves to a greater extent.

The main difference between this system and modern slavery is the fact that labor-intensive production now tends to take place more or less in the same areas where "enslavable" people live, greatly reducing or even eliminating the initial investment costs—slavery today is cheap. Slaves are normally not purchased, but controlled either psychologically or through violence. Legal ownership brings responsibility and is therefore mostly shunned. Also, there is little or no incentive for the maintenance of slaves. There are plenty more where they came from and it is inexpensive to get them. If a modern slave becomes sick, injured, or pregnant, he or she is simply thrown out and replaced by someone else. Slaves have become disposable.

Inspired by Bales, we suggest the following five criteria to determine whether child labor can be called slavery:

1. The child produces an economic profit.
2. The child is controlled psychologically.
3. The child works because of the use or the fear of violence.
4. The child is not paid.
5. The child has few or no opportunities to escape.

The first three criteria are present in many, perhaps even the majority, of child labor situations. Children are easy to exploit through manipulation and psychological control mechanisms. They are also so inexperienced that they have no choice but to trust the adults around them. On the

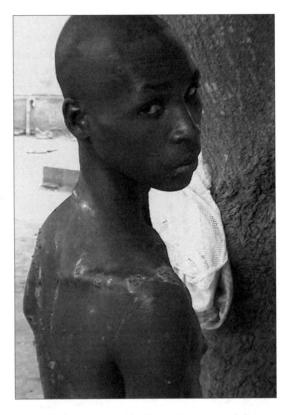

Brian Edwards of True Vision took this picture of a boy who escaped from a cocoa farm in Côte d'Ivoire. While some of the boy's wounds stem from maltreatment, others are most likely the result of applying pesticides and agrochemicals without wearing proper protection. His outward injuries could thus be short-term, but his exposure to toxic chemicals may have caused long-term damage to his central nervous system and fertility.

other hand, corporal punishment is so common in Africa that we must assume that a large share of working children fear the consequences of opposing their employer. The experience of a Malian boy discussed earlier is probably typical of many cases of exploitative child labor.[62]

When he arrived at the coffee farm, another boy told him about a child who tried to escape but was caught and badly beaten. The boy had not seen this himself, but some other workers had told him. It is difficult to know whether the story was true, since none of the boys in question had in fact witnessed what had happened. The important point, however, was that they all believed the account and the fear of a brutal punishment kept them working at the farm.

It is the fourth and fifth criteria listed above that seriously limit the group of exploited children whom we would call slaves. Apart from the children who work for their own family and relatives, most working children earn a salary, no matter how unfair, or at least there exists some kind of agreement about how they will be paid. But there are gray zones. Employers may save the salaries on behalf of the children, or they may agree to pay the children at the end of a season or service period. These engagements are not always honored. Some children run away, losing not only their "saved" earnings but also their possessions. Others are fired for reasons that are not always legitimate. When something is missing in a household, the child domestic servant is often blamed and either the value of the missing item is deducted from the child's savings, or the child is dismissed unpaid.

Very few child workers in Africa are actually locked up and therefore physically prevented from running away. Can some of them still qualify as slaves? As mentioned, the employer is often the keeper of the child's salary. This makes the cost of running away extremely high and may in many cases deprive the children of any opportunity to pay their way back home. When working far away from their parents and kin, where would they go? Life in the streets is rough in many African cities, and we have even seen cases where children enter into unpaid servitude just to have a safe place to sleep. Also, in the case of children, deciding whether there is a realistic chance of escape is even more complicated, because psychological walls are sometimes much more difficult to climb than physical ones. The self-esteem of children who are systematically punished and repeatedly told how worthless they are may sink so low that they begin to think that they deserve what is done to them and even develop the belief that they are stupid and worthless and therefore lucky to be in an exploitative situation.[63] Fear of violence, combined with threats like "You cannot hide from me, I'll find you, wherever you go" may not impress an adult, but it will scare a child. If we add threats of witchcraft and curses, we see that the employers of children have a wide repertoire of virtual handcuffs to draw from.

One sensitive question remains unavoidable on a continent where the great majority of children work for their own families or kin. Can parents be accused of enslaving their own children? The five criteria for slavery will inevitably be fulfilled in numerous cases of family-controlled child labor. Parents no doubt have a great influence over their children and over their children's own perception of what they should accept. What right do parents have to force their children to work for free? Or to put it in the words of the African Charter, to *what extent* do children have the obligation to work for the cohesion of their family?

While some may doubt the legitimacy of saying that parents can possibly use their own children as slaves, we have certainly seen some cases where few other descriptions seem adequate. The question remains extremely complicated in cases where children work within the family unit, while it is clearer in cases where parents rent out their children to do dangerous work and keep the earnings for themselves. The worst cases are obviously the ones where the parents sell their own children into prostitution.

Orphans, AIDS, and Child Labor

When one or both parents die, children are often left in the care—and at the mercy—of the extended family. If the extended family is unable or unwilling to help, or if it cannot be located, children will generally have to fend for themselves. Because of AIDS, the number of such children has steadily increased over the past decade, although the orphan *rate* has stabilized in most African countries. It is estimated that in 2003, there were 43.4 million orphans in Africa (or 12.3 percent of children age 18 and under), 7.7 million of them having lost both their parents. While 28 percent of all orphans have lost their parents to AIDS, as many as 59 percent of double-orphaned children have. With only 10 percent of the world's population, Africa thus has more than 90 percent of the world's AIDS orphans.[64]

Most double-orphans are placed in the households of relatives, and even orphans who have lost only one parent will often not go on living with the one who remains: while 46 percent of the motherless children do not live with their fathers, 28 percent of the fatherless children stay with people other than their mothers. The fact that fatherless orphans are more likely to stay with the remaining parent is quite consistent for the twenty-six countries under discussion here. Only in Niger, Nigeria, Guinea, and Togo does the gender of the surviving parent seem to be unimportant in determining who the child stays with.[65] Single-parent orphans are twice as likely as nonorphans to live with their grandparents, and three times as likely to live in a household headed by another relative.[66] Who that relative is, matters greatly.

In some cultures it is common for the father's family to demand custody of the children after the father's death, sometimes through forced marriage between the widow and one of her husband's brothers.[67] In some of the cases where the children remain with their mother, the mother loses her property, including her home, to the father's relatives, leaving her destitute and with little choice but to demand a much greater contribution from the children's work.[68] If she's lucky, the widow only loses the income that was provided by her husband. She is then forced to work harder and longer, often leaving the children with the burden of household chores. Should she remarry, the children will most likely be placed with her relatives, as many men resent living with the offspring of another man in their household.

While some men choose to keep the children upon their wife's death, it is common to entrust at least the younger children to an aunt or grandmother on the father's side of the family. In the majority of the cases, however, children who lose their mother end up living with a stepmother, either because the father remarries or because he was in a polygamous union to begin with. As stepchildren they will tend to be discriminated against, Cinderella style, with much harsher treatment and certainly with much more work than the other children in the household. Boys who have lost their mother may be at particular risk, because they rank above the children of the second wife with regard to inheritance. The fear of harm from the second wife, eager to protect the rights of her own children, is a much quoted reason to send maternally orphaned boys to live away from home.

In most African cultures, the father's family has the responsibility for—and the right to—his children. Double-orphaned children are likewise the responsibility of the family of the child's father. However, the interest in an orphaned child is not always based exclusively on care and duty. Several reports from southern Africa mention relatives taking in children for commercial gain, either from their labor or from grants made available to orphan caregivers by well-meaning assistance programs.[69]

Another option for double-orphaned children is to remain in their original household, sometimes with elderly relatives. In these cases older siblings, and particularly girls, take over the parents' responsibility for younger siblings, leaving them with less time and resources to invest in their own education and careers. The elderly can be both a resource and a burden. Grandparents may be able to provide the children with protection, supervision, and love. On the other hand, the elderly may also be, or become, a source of additional work for the children, since they will eventually need both care and support.

Needless to say, double-orphaned children left to fend for themselves are extremely vulnerable. Researchers in Zambia were surprised by the extent to which they found orphans engaged in physically demanding, dangerous, and sexually abusive work—and how they were regularly exploited in those situations.[70]

An unusually thorough study by Anne Case, Christina Paxson, and

When parents die, children are often left without a home and with the burden of providing not only for themselves, but also for elderly relatives.

Joseph Ableidinger has given a fairly accurate picture of the living arrangements and life situation of orphans in Ghana, Kenya, Malawi, Mozambique, Namibia, Niger, Tanzania, Uganda, Zambia, and Zimbabwe. Using large datasets from household surveys, the study has been able to point out some general trends with a fair amount of certainty. While earlier studies indicated that orphans tend to live in poorer households than children in general, these researchers find that this is only true for children who lose their father.[71] They even find that double-orphans live in slightly better-off households than nonorphans, something that contradicts previous theories.[72] Perhaps more important to our topic, they find that orphans in all of the countries examined are more likely to live in households that are headed by a woman or an illiterate person, and that have a higher proportion of elderly members. These three factors are commonly associated with increased child labor.

Because children mostly live and work in the sphere of women, and because women provide children with more support than do men, it makes a big difference to an orphan which parent he or she loses. Though children who lose their father are more likely to live in poorer households, we also know that household assets are a poor predictor of children's labor participation. In fact, we can assume that men will be more likely to invest in household durables like TVs and refrigerators, while women will be more prone to prioritize the children's needs. As well, household expenditures for child-related goods like nutritious food and health services are more likely to drop if the mother dies.[73]

We have little information on how the loss of a parent affects child labor directly. Preliminary results from the analysis of household data collected by UNICEF in four countries (Burundi, Côte d'Ivoire, Malawi, and Senegal) suggest that, by and large, orphans are more likely to work than nonorphans, but there is no definite pattern—sometimes this is true only for maternal orphans, other times only for girls, and in Senegal there appears to be almost no difference. On the other hand, there is relatively good information on how orphanhood affects children's schooling. The school attendance rate of orphans as a percentage of that of nonorphans is, for instance, around 80 percent if we look at the average for twenty-eight sub-Saharan African countries. An interesting exception is Guinea Bissau, where orphans have higher school attendance rates than nonorphans, but the general trend is the opposite: the absolutely worst situation is found in Mozambique, where orphans have a school attendance rate that is only 47 percent of the rate for nonorphans, followed by Ethiopia with a respective rate of 60 percent.[74] In the countries in Case, Paxson, and Ableidinger's study, orphans were also found to be considerably much less likely to go to school—on average 11 percent less likely than their peers—and the effect was equal for boys and girls.[75] Perhaps most interesting, and supporting our previous claims, this study found that maternal orphans suffer a larger drop in schooling rates than do paternal orphans, even if paternal orphans live in poorer households. Double-orphans—who were in fact found to live in households that are slightly better off than those of both single-parent orphans and nonorphaned children—are much less likely to attend school than both paternal and maternal orphans, which is additional evidence showing how household wealth fails to give good indications about child schooling and labor participation rates.

A well-functioning extended family system is in many ways a complex insurance mechanism that above all helps to smooth income variability for its members. While one part of the family is in trouble, the other parts help out—for instance, by temporarily hosting children—

until the dysfunctional unit is back on its feet. The AIDS epidemic is putting a strain on the capacity of extended families to play their insurance role. Particularly in southern and eastern Africa, several units within the same family system are hit simultaneously, leaving the remaining productive adults with an unbearably high number of people to support. This often means that family members who would under normal conditions be net-consumers, like children and the elderly, are forced to become net-contributors.

Either because the extended family abandons orphaned children, or because the children themselves run away from an overwhelming burden of responsibility or exploitation by the foster parents, a large number of orphaned children are destined to end up with no support at all, either economically or emotionally. Until recently, parents or close relatives employed the majority of the working children in Africa. The AIDS epidemic, however, has resulted in a considerable shift in the number of children who offer their services in the open labor market.[76] This further worsens the negotiating power of working children, creating ideal conditions for the most merciless exploitation and pushing many children to take up life in the street and possibly turn to crime in a desperate quest for survival.

PART I

CHILDREN AT WORK

Introduction to Part I

THE AIR HAS BECOME HEAVY WITH HEAT. LIKE A HOT BLANKET BETWEEN us and the sky, which by now looks hopelessly distant and faint, smothering plants, animals, and humans. In the midday sun there is a stillness that calls for quiet conversations and afternoon naps. Under the mango tree we long for some breeze, watching its leaves to glimpse the faintest rustling that will announce a waft of wind. It is time for a break. Our assistant Martine muses: "I was thinking as I was translating that, in fact, none of the languages we speak have exact expressions describing what I think you refer to when you talk about *child labor.* The closest I get are terms describing *the type of work that children do,* or *work suitable for children,* but none of them imply that it is bad. Then of course there are words describing child maltreatment and slavery, but that would be something else." Martine's observation was echoed in a May 17, 2002, BBC interview with Alice Ouedrago, director for policy development at the ILO and herself an African: "The concepts we use to talk about child labor, when you look at the many languages in Africa, [do] not convey any negative perceptions, it seems to be all right."

So what types of work are considered to be "suitable for children"? Children's work needs to be fairly simple and should preferably not require much adult supervision. Apart from these two factors, the type of work children do reflects the basic needs and demand structures of African countries. The most fundamental necessities are, of course, food and water. Consequently, the greatest share of African child labor deals with producing and preparing food and, above all, fetching water. Water is needed not only in the household, but also for farming, gardening, raising animals, construction, and panning for gold. Thus, water provision is one of the main responsibilities of children working in a variety of sectors. Because construction material is another basic need, it is common to find children occupied in brickyards, at construction sites, and in the production of gravel in quarries. Typical African apprenticeships also seem to reflect the spending priorities of low- and middle-income men and women. Men tend to care deeply for their cars and mopeds, and we consequently find a great number of garages where the mechanic employs young boys as apprentices. Women are inclined to

Children selling bags in the market is a common sight throughout Africa. Is it "work suitable for children"?

spend more on their appearance, resulting in a myriad of tailoring and hairdressing shops where many girl apprentices are also found.

Part 1 of this book takes a closer look at some of the most typical labor chores of African children. These can be divided into four main groups: the first includes the tasks that most African children perform *in and around their own households,* mainly supervised by their own parents or close relatives. The second focuses on work that is frequently referred to as *apprenticeship,* although the craftsmen tend to take full economic advantage of the labor supply their young apprentices can provide. The third group comprises activities in the *commercial labor market,* where children's work does not pretend to have a cultural or pedagogical value—it is simply work. The last group describes some of the so-called *worst forms of child labor.* The children performing these types of activities may not be numerous compared to groups of other working children, but the extreme harmfulness of their situation demands that we give them special attention.

Child labor performed within the control of the family is normally portrayed as relatively harmless and less worthy of policy intervention. However, because the many elements that make child labor harmful (listed in Chapter 1 of this book) can easily be found in home-based work, there is a high incidence of hazard within this category. Moreover, older children, in particular, are often frustrated within home-based work situations because of limited freedom and because they don't get to control any of the income their work helps generate.

It is the so-called worst forms of child labor, rather than child labor abuses within the home, that shock the general public. Because these forms of child exploitation are so outrageous, the media and activists frequently pick them first to illustrate the horrors of child labor, giving

Child labor in Africa mainly reflects the most basic needs of African families, like the use of firewood, to make charcoal, to cook food, and to provide warmth.

an impression of the child labor situation that is far from representative. It is true that child soldiers often are abducted children, child prostitutes are often trafficked, and street children are often orphaned or abandoned.

But these generalizations miss important details. Based on our research and document review, we can only conclude that children—even in dire circumstances—often *do* have a will of their own, and in many cases do influence the decisions concerning their own lives. Many child soldiers are in fact self-recruited. Many street children are runaways and do have families, but have chosen to abandon misery, domestic conflict, or abuse (Bozari 2003). Many girls occasionally or regularly choose to take money for sex in order to provide themselves with the little luxuries they would otherwise never be able to purchase, or to put themselves through school. And a great majority of the children intercepted in trafficking in West Africa explain that they were in fact eager to go (See UNICEF 1999b). Failing to realize this diversity will inevitably give policy designers and programmers quite a surprise when they reach the field. It is likely to produce projects that are less relevant and less efficient than they could be (see Castle and Diarra 2003). In the pages that follow, we have consequently tried to break away from some of these stereotypes, and our examples have been chosen accordingly.

While the chapters in Part 1 are meant to describe the work most frequently done by children throughout Africa, it is obvious that our account is in no way exhaustive. In particular, some tasks may be very common in one country or city but rare or absent in another. This is the case of South Africa's "taxi children" (who clean taxis at the car stations); Kenya's "child conductors" (who assist the drivers of public minibuses in seating passengers, loading their luggage, and looking out for clients and obstacles); and Addis Ababa's "shoeshine boys" (many of whom are extraordinarily well organized and run their own savings unions). Nor is our account exclusive, in the sense that a given child may only perform one task. African children typically do many things, combining, for instance, household work and street vending; street vendors sometimes also sell sex, child soldiers also cook, and street children tend to do almost anything for money. Moreover, many children in the commercial labor market change work frequently. Our aim is to show these distinctions and thus, if possible, help provide a less black-and-white picture of the African child labor situation.

2

Child Labor in and Around the Household

MOST AFRICAN CHILDREN START TO WORK AT AN EARLY AGE. BY THE TIME they are 3 or 4 years old, their contribution in the household is needed and expected, however small it may be. Busy mothers will often start by sending their young ones to fetch things, first within the household, and later in the neighborhood or village or at the market. On our way to a meeting in a small town one morning, we noticed how certain children appeared to be busy going from place to place, carrying various objects with a responsible look in their eyes that said, "I have a mission to accomplish." While teaching small children to carry out simple instructions is a universal pedagogical practice, African kids are more likely to learn by carrying out instructions that result in saving time for an adult who works in and around the household.

Unpaid work in and around the household probably constitutes as much as 90 percent of the labor of African children if we include work on the family farm. This is mainly due to limited industrialization and an underdeveloped commercial labor market in which large groups of unemployed adults stand first in line for wage-earning opportunities. In the relatively few cases where employers prefer children to adults, the labor offered often has a nature, status, and salary level that adults would be unlikely to accept.

But what exactly do children do? Time allocation studies from countries as different as Benin, Botswana, Ethiopia, Sudan, Tanzania, and Zimbabwe provide a fairly consistent picture in terms of the types of activities carried out by African children.[1] On the other hand, the average amount of time devoted to different tasks reflects national

57

specificities. Herding, for example, occupies Botswana's boys more than others, because of the importance of beef production in that country.

Figures 2.1a and 2.1b show the most common work activities of children ages 6 to 14 in urban and rural Benin, respectively. Though the data are specific to Benin, they are probably representative of many places in Africa, with one exception: the tables reflect a dry season and therefore do not account for the extensive time that African children spend on farm work in general.

Those who have traveled in the African countryside and are familiar with the sight of children carrying buckets on their heads will not be surprised to learn that fetching water is the most time-consuming task for rural children, both boys and girls. Much has been written about the burden that fetching water represents for women all over the developing world, but much less about the burden it represents for children. Yet its importance cannot be overstressed. An anecdote illustrates the point: About ten years ago, we were surprised to find an exceptionally high rate of school attendance in a remote Togolese village. We looked for the conditions that usually explain such success stories—relatively well-

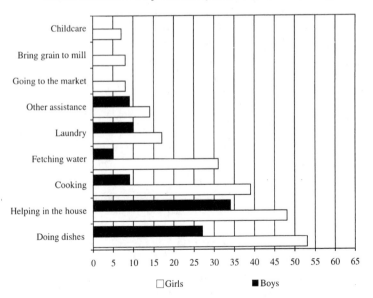

Figure 2.1a   Participation in labor tasks in Benin, urban children 6–14 years old (percentage participating)

Source: UNDP 1998.

**Figure 2.1b   Participation in labor tasks in Benin,
rural children 6–14 years old (percentage participating)**

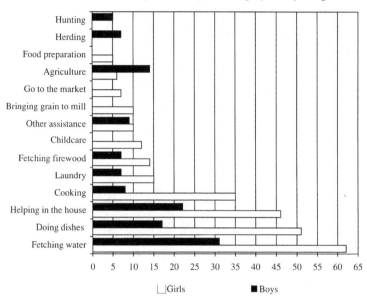

Source: UNDP 1998.

schooled mothers, active NGOs, inspired leaders, committed missionar-
ies, excellent teachers, effective media campaigns. We found none of it.
The explanation came from the school principal: in this village the water
was so far away—more than twelve hours in the dry season—that children of primary school age could not be used to fetch it. So they were
going to school instead.[2]

Doing dishes is the most time-consuming task for urban children,
and the second most time-consuming for rural girls. One reason why it
may take so much time is that meals are often served to a large number
of people, and that the dishes must be carried to a water source for
washing because it is easier to take the dishes to the water than to carry
home all the water needed to do a good job. The third most time-consuming activity for rural girls is helping out around the house by doing a
variety of small tasks and errands (remember that children often are
socialized into being available to assist adults in the household), while
activities revolving around food (going to the mill or market, pounding
or grinding, cooking) take up considerable time for girls. A 13-year-old
girl in Zimbabwe describes her day very much in accordance with
Figure 2.1b:

Food preparation and washing dishes are among the most time-demanding household chores for African girls.

Today I went to wash plates in the morning. Before I even left for school, and after I had dried the plates, I started grinding sorghum. When I came from school I cooked sadza [white maize porridge, the staple food in Zimbabwe] for my brother and myself. After eating I went to wash plates again. When I came from washing plates I went to grind. After grinding I fetched water from the stream for my brothers to wash, and for my father also.[3]

In the area where we gathered our data, only the boys turned out to herd and hunt, and were more often involved in agriculture than were the girls. However, girls also tend smaller animals in many African countries.

Subsistence Agriculture

Throughout African literature, *going to farm* is evoked with a mix of pain and longing. Farming together is a joint struggle for survival, giving a strong feeling of belonging and strengthening group solidarity. In some places, farming together is a lifestyle and an important part of what it means to be a family. For example, a rice-growing family in Uganda will leave the household for months at a time to live in temporary shelters near their farm, where they can watch over and care for the rice paddies. When necessary, they will spend hours chasing away birds from the crop by using a homemade wooden device that shoots small clay bullets that have been carefully and massively produced by women and children during the daytime for this particular purpose. It may sound exotic to non-Africans, but it is not unusual that a farming family will find it necessary to stay up all night to defend their crops from, for instance, hippopotami or elephants trampling the fields and eating and ruining a year's work in the span of a few hours.

It is not only normal but also suitable that children work on the family farm, because there they learn techniques and skills that are important for their future survival, firmly anchored in the family solidarity network. Of course, there are also economic considerations. When land is abundant, child labor availability, particularly in peak seasons, turns out to be what decides the ceiling for household production, and represents the "adjustable labor" of an otherwise altruistic family.[4] In general, as suggested by the wealth paradox (see Chapter 1), when a household possesses labor-demanding assets such as land and livestock, children are more likely to work, because the alternative costs of leisure and schooling increase. A study of rural time allocation carried out in Botswana concluded that the more productive capital the household has, the more productive work its children perform.[5] Another study from rural Ethiopia went one step further and found that while some assets are indeed child labor–demanding, others are child labor–saving. Based on a systematic analysis of the impact of various household assets on child labor rates, the Ethiopian study concluded that owning small livestock and controlling farmland increase the demand for child labor, while owning assets like oxen, bulls, and plows decreases it.[6]

While the above findings are based on reasonable interpretations of the way African households relate to the labor resources of their children, it is also true that many—if not most—rural households appear to use child labor in a rather inefficient way. This inevitably increases child labor demand beyond what is necessary. To understand why this is so, a number of recent studies stress that, in many cases, a rural household can hardly be seen as one consolidated economic unit: it rather resembles a bargaining model in which the various household members all have their individual agenda.[7] Assuming "efficient" pooling of income, labor resources and responsibilities are not always the norm. Often, various adult household members have their own plots, yielding their own personal incomes, and tend to have separately defined economic responsibilities, sometimes with little interest left for the household as a whole.[8] In addition, there is evidence of low trust between household members, in some cases even leading to a commercialization of the relationship between spouses. In Togo, wives have been observed selling water to their husbands, and in Senegal, husbands are known to sell firewood to their wives.[9] Such lack of unity and pooling might in fact make maximization of the overall outcome for the household relatively irrelevant to the individual member.

The use of children's labor is a good illustration of this apparent inefficiency in some households. Men tend to have plots with better soil, which are generally used to grow cash crops. To be overall efficient, therefore, the household labor force should logically concentrate on the men's plots in order to obtain the maximum return to the household unit.[10] However, since the men control the income from their plots, women often prefer to spend time working on their own, often less productive, cash crop or subsistence plots, which often have poorer soil quality and, moreover, mainly produce subsistence products, something that would normally lead to a joint productivity loss for the household. When women work on men's land, they sometimes do a poorer job. In Kenya, where women weed the men's maize crops, the productivity increase as a result of weeding was found to differ markedly between male- and female-headed households, giving much better returns in the cases where women controlled the income of the farm.[11] To the extent to which women are in charge of the children's labor, the children may also be more likely to work on the less-productive plots of their mothers.[12]

Based on available anthropological literature, there is reason to believe that children also have at least some influence on whose land to farm, beyond mere customary claims.[13] They therefore also affect the productivity of their own labor, in the sense that they choose both which plot to work and what effort to exert. Pamela Reynolds observed that Tonga children in Zimbabwe even have their own "experimental" plots, which they tend to farm inefficiently due to insufficient adult supervision. She observed how children appear to allocate their farm labor strategically, either for immediate benefits or to strengthen future alliances. As an example, girls may voluntarily work on their brothers'

At least 80 percent of African child labor is related to subsistence agriculture. The more farmland a peasant family has, the more likely it is that the children of the household will work.

plots, because should they have problems with their future husbands, their brothers will be the most likely source of help.[14]

In Chapter 1 we discussed the implications of the African Charter's perception of a mutuality between children's rights and children's duties in the African household. By presenting rights, such as care and food, as rewards for duties, such as working for the family, the charter in fact sees children as active decisionmakers. That the strategic labor allocation choice of children may actually worsen the overall outcome for the household unit may not mean much to the children themselves as long as they are empowered to improve their own welfare through their labor choices.

Childcare

Open fires, boiling water, and uncovered wells make the typical African household a dangerous place for toddlers. As anyone who has looked after young kids knows, accidents can happen in the blink of an eye, making it unreasonable to simultaneously do anything requiring concentration or continuity. With no childcare facilities in the village and plenty of work for women to do, it is no wonder that the responsibility for childcare ends up on the shoulders of older sisters and brothers. Often not much older, though. In rural Botswana, girls between 7 and 9 years of age were found to spend twice as much time on childcare than did girls and women of any other age group.[15] When a new child is born, the second youngest, often as young as 1 or 2, is commonly passed on to the care of the other children in the household. Throughout Africa, it is not unusual to see children as young as 5 or 6 carrying an even younger child on their back. Having their younger brother or sister strapped to their back will certainly reduce the infant's risk of accidents and, perhaps more important, buy themselves some freedom of movement and enough control to direct their attention to something else.

Childcare is a primary example of the type of task by which children substitute for women in African households, enabling their mothers to be occupied with something else within or outside the household. With an average of almost six children per woman, women's productivity would be strongly reduced if they could not delegate babysitting to some of their older offspring—preferably those still too young to be able to do more strenuous or difficult tasks. As it is, women can pursue their farm activities more freely, do household chores more effectively, take their products to the market, and especially in urban areas, run their businesses outside the house.

While learning to look after younger siblings is probably good experience that makes children feel both valued and "big," it can, like most child labor activities, be overdone. Despite their best intentions, children with protracted babysitting responsibilities are likely to become distracted, sometimes with dire consequences for their younger sibling and also, by the end of the day, harsh punishment for the babysitter child.

The extent to which childcare ends up on children's shoulders and how it affects their welfare is a function of several factors: at a practical level, it is a question of the availability of other potential babysitters, like healthy and willing grandparents, domestic servants, or even day-care arrangements. At an economic level, the important factors are often the mother's share of financial responsibility in the household and the

Childcare is a typical example of children taking over the mother's responsibilities, giving her the possibility to do higher-return work within or outside the household.

opportunity costs were she to take a greater portion of the babysitting responsibility herself. At a psychological level, the personal ambition of the mother versus her altruism toward the working child is a key factor. The latter two are closely linked. It is both understandable and legitimate when a poor mother leaves the responsibility for her toddler to an older child so that she can grow food for the whole family.[16] However, what is a need to one person may be a luxury—or at least an option—to someone else. Some mothers may decide to work extra hard to buy shoes for their children, others may consider that flip-flops are enough, and others still may see no problem with barefooted children, especially if this means being able to take a well-deserved break.

The distribution of household chores like childcare is a clear-cut example of a situation where the mother and her children tend to have conflicting interests—her professional ambition against their schooling needs, her freedom to visit friends against their freedom to play. Unfortunately, having to look after younger siblings is still a much cited reason for not sending girls to school, and in many cases an older girl is "sacrificed" to help her mother, freeing up her brothers' and sisters' time so that they can go to school. In other cases childcare needs result in the household acquiring a child domestic servant.

Fetching Water

Water is perhaps the most fundamental problem of African households. The problem is not just where to obtain potable water, but also its transportation. In many places the water sources are a long distance from the consumers—especially in the dry season, when cisterns, ponds, wells, and rivers tend to dry up. It is no coincidence that in areas where someone can afford a cart, a beast of burden, or some other means of transport, water distribution is quickly commercialized.

Fetching water is a simple but physically demanding task generally assigned to women and children. Considerable research has been done on the time that women spend fetching water, but far less on the time spent by children. Even very young children will go with their mother to the water source, first on her back and later following her on foot. Bringing the children is practical for other reasons than just looking after them. Washing the children at the water source saves the considerable amount of time that would be required to transport the water home. And even young kids can carry some water. By the age of 4, many children have already transported a considerable amount of water, although in small buckets. While it may seem discriminatory that men so rarely participate in this heavy and time-consuming job, it clearly also has its practical sides. Women can feel much freer to carry out intimate washing of their bodies in a place where men rarely go, and water sources become important centers for exchanging information, gossiping, and bonding with other women.

Apart from the obvious health and development implications of the time and energy children spend on "water duty," there is another problem: fetching water is an inflexible need that conflicts with schooling, in particular for girls. To better understand the importance of this issue, let's imagine a village of 1,000 inhabitants in rural Benin. Based on the demographic distribution in rural areas, we will find 300 children between 6 and 14 years old in the village.[17] Among them are 138 girls and 162 boys, and according to education statistics, 21 of the girls and 52 of the boys will be attending school. Let's also conservatively estimate that 25 percent of the rest of the population are inactive because they are too young (under 6), too old, ill, or disabled. That leaves 230 women between the ages of 15 and 49, and 220 men in the same age group. Based on time allocation data, we can calculate how many hours per week are spent fetching water by children who go to school, children who don't, and adults (15–49 years old),[18] as shown in Figure 2.2.

Figure 2.2 Hours spent fetching water per week in Benin by age and gender

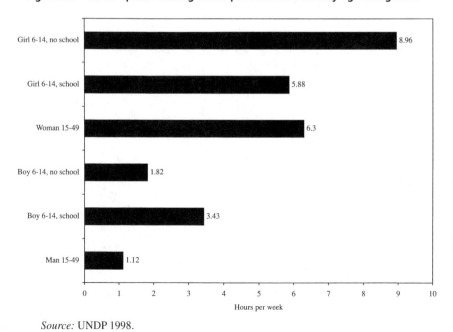

Source: UNDP 1998.

Like most of her peers, this 8-year-old girl fetches water every day. She is on her way to the lake, but because of the drought, there is very little water. She uses a small calabash to fill the basin. Providing villages with water would dramatically reduce the child labor demand in Africa.

As expected, fetching water takes up much more time for women and girls than for men and boys, and it is primarily a children's task.

Multiplying the number of individuals in each age/gender/schooling status group by the hours children in each group spend fetching water, we find that the people in our average village would spend 3,196 hours on water duty in the course of an average week; 1,500 of these hours would be child labor, 1,109 of them performed by girls.

Now let's imagine that a central water pump and a couple of wells were constructed in the village. While this would not save all the time spent fetching water, it would certainly help a great deal—let's say 80 percent. We have then saved a total of 2,557 hours of work weekly, including 1,200 hours of child work, 931 of them girls' work. We have seen that only a few children in the village go to school, and that most of them are boys. The children who do go to school spend on average a total of 23 hours a week on their studies, including school and home-work time. Converting into school hours the time saved by children who no longer have to walk to a distant water source, we find that 52 more children could be sent to school, almost doubling the attendance rate (if only the girls were to benefit from the improved accessibility of water, their school attendance rate would almost triple). Now let's also assume that half the time that adults spent fetching water was fungible, and that adults would now use some of their saved time to do some of the other chores commonly done by children. This could increase the number of children going to school by 111, reaching a total of 184, which would almost triple the initial overall school attendance (again, if only the girls in our village were to benefit from adults taking over some of the chil-dren's chores, this would practically give all the girls enough time to go to school).

Assuming 80 percent substitution of water fetching time with schooling time may sound unrealistic. On the other hand, we could also extend the calculation to include time saved on other water-demanding tasks, like washing dishes and doing the laundry, knowing that some of the time spent on such tasks accounts for the trip to and from the water source. In our typical Beninese village, 853 hours are spent washing dishes each week and 1,153 on doing laundry. Since these tasks demand less walking time and more active labor time by the water source, the time saved would be considerably less than for fetching water. However, even with a timesaving of just 25 percent, 22 more children could be sent to school.

These calculations leave no doubt that if children did not have to spend time fetching water, school attendance could increase dramatical-ly, especially for girls, and child labor could be greatly reduced. We believe, however, that interventions aimed at reducing child labor by providing water need to be well targeted and accompanied by communi-cation exercises to raise awareness about the importance of schooling. If not, it is quite likely that stronger players than children will walk away with the main benefits of the time saved.

Fetching Firewood

A bit away from our mango tree a young boy is passing with a huge load of firewood, walking along the dust road, not too fast and not too slow. In the midday heat you save your energy and search for a balance between what your body can take without hurting too much and your urge to get back home and finally unload the burden. As our assistant Martine gets up and walks over to the boy, he stops, looking shy and alert at the same time, but he seems to be a polite child and receives us, foreign women, with a submissive glance. Would he be willing to talk? Martine helps him lift the branches from his head. I ask if I can try to carry it, like he does, on my head. Now he smiles, puzzled. I kneel down, and with Martine's help he lifts up the firewood and places it on my head. Struggling to keep my balance, I stand up, noticing how the muscles in the neck strain as they try to balance and sustain the surprisingly heavy load. I take a few steps, with the small branches piercing my scalp, and feel how my head hurts under the pressure of the heavy logs. With my hand I try to find a place to support the load, but wherever I reach the tiny branches sting me. Probably little more than a minute passes before I have to ask for help to get the firewood off my head. Laughter is coming from under the mango tree. But this 10-year-old carries this load all the way to his destination, walking for miles in the heat—perhaps every day.

Where was he going? We did not ask him. There and then it did not

Where is he going? If the firewood is for sale or for his father's workshop, his work will be considered an economic activity and this will count as child labor in official statistics. If the firewood is for private household use, this type of work will not qualify as child labor.

seem important. What seemed important was the heavy load, the heat, and the long and dusty road. However, his destination is important to the academic debate, and yet again shows how difficult it is to give a clear-cut definition of child labor. In the ILO's global estimate of child labor, work is defined in terms of "economic activity,"[19] which does not cover children engaged in domestic chores within their own households. Also, international labor standards provide an exception for such chores within the child's own household.[20]

So, in fact, it does matter where the boy was going. If he was taking firewood to the market to sell, he was clearly involved in an economic activity. If his father was a smith, and he was taking the firewood to his father's workshop, he would also be counted in the child labor statistics. However, if he was taking the firewood home so that his mother could heat the family's dinner—well, his hardship would no longer be counted. Fetching firewood is a strong illustration of how difficult it is to define, measure, and assess child labor issues in Africa. As is fetching water: If a girl takes water to her father for his cattle, she is considered economically active, and thus officially a child laborer. If she takes water to her mother for household work, she is not.

Herding

Children often end up doing work that adults don't like. Herding is a typical example. Despite what Western movies would have us believe, it is a lonely and tedious job that requires no particular skill or strength, so it is an ideal job to leave to children. Possibly because cattle tending takes one away from the household-controlled sphere, and because it can generate considerable amounts of cash, it is almost exclusively a male business—women keep chickens and goats, but rarely more than one or two cows. Most child herders across Africa, therefore, are boys.

In places where animal husbandry is a major source of income, it is normal that boys spend the majority of their labor time tending cattle. In the rural areas of Botswana, one of Africa's main exporters of beef, boys between 10 and 14 years old spend an average of almost seven hours a day herding cattle, and even younger boys put some five hours a day into herding (see Figure 2.3).[21] Considering that cattle need tending seven days a week, while school is in session only five days a week, it is easy to see how, for instance, Tswana boys spend far more time in the company of cows than in the company of books.

In addition to being a lonely job most unlikely to stimulate children's creativity, herding has two other drawbacks. One is the well-

**Figure 2.3   Hours spent herding per day
in Botswana by age and gender**

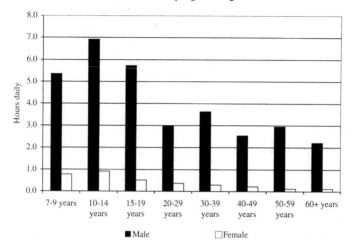

Source: Mueller 1984.

founded fear of snakes and other wild animals. The other is the stress caused by being responsible for significant value (the cattle) at a young age. The boys must remain constantly alert and are left with little time and opportunity to play and rest, even when several of them are working together.

Zeleke Takele, a 12-year-old, tells of his experience as a herder for a large estate owner in the hills of North Gondar in Ethiopia:

My mother stays at home and my father is a day laborer. Neither one of them can read or write. I started to work when I was 11, so this is my first year working. My parents sent me to work for a rich peasant family to look after their cattle. What else could I do? I decided to work. I start work at 6 in the morning. I go to the pastures with the animals and I'm back home in the evening at 6:30. I work the whole week including weekends and holidays. Back when I was living with my master's family, they only gave me lunch and dinner. Now they pay me with 90 kilos of grain per year. What I earn, I give to my parents. But the payment is not fair because I get paid less than a grown-up and I do the same work. I tend cattle on the open field, and it takes me about 30 minutes to walk from my parents' place to the field. The work is no good. It can be very cold in the morning and evening, and very hot during the day. Sometimes it rains, and animals have attacked me. My boss yells at me and beats me, and I often get sick. There is no school, no play and no one to talk to, and I miss my family. I don't like my work because it is hard. I work for many hours with nowhere to go to get away from the sun, the rain, the dust and the snakes. No time to play with my friends, no rest. And no chance of learning anything. Above all, I feel sorry for myself for not going to school like my friends. I would have liked to go to school if it had been possible.[22]

One thing is common among most stories we have heard from young herders: the fear of snakes. This Peuhl boy and his little friends are always alert, since not only snakes but also lions are common in the area where they work. Herding is one of the types of labor that adults around the world are most reluctant to do.

3

Child Labor as Apprenticeship Arrangement

AT TIMES IT IS HARD TO SEPARATE APPRENTICESHIP FROM PURE ECONOMIC exploitation of children.[1] However, compared to regular commercial work, apprenticeship arrangements should have two basic distinguishing features. First, the overarching objective of an apprenticeship should be to learn a marketable trade. Since apprentices are students, they are not paid for their supposed educational labor. On the contrary, it is not uncommon that parents pay the artisan to train the child, and that apprentices pay a "liberation fee" when they are ready to leave their master and start on their own. The second feature distinguishing apprenticeships from regular commercial work is the long-term perspective of the apprenticeship arrangement. The young apprentices are often placed in more or less regular foster care with their instructors, and this tends to result in a relationship between student and master that encompasses much more than training.

To learn a craft is the dream of many African children who never made it to school or who dropped out. For a boy to be a mechanic or a carpenter, and for a girl to be a hairdresser or a tailor, may indeed be a ticket to future income. Considering the quality of schooling in many African countries and the bleak labor market prospects for many of those with a formal education, completing an apprenticeship may look like a much better investment than finishing primary or secondary school. Moreover, a family may see it as poor management of meager funds to send *all* the children to school to get the same education. Choosing different educations for children, with some pursuing formal education and others learning various trades, spreads risk. Besides,

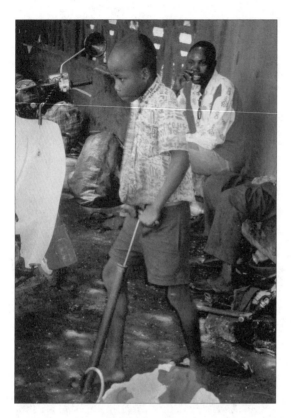

Apprenticeship is primarily meant to teach the child a craft. Many parents pay for an apprenticeship, and sometimes the child must pay a "liberation fee" to conclude the learning period. Child apprentices are often used to conduct the most menial work for the tutor, work that often has little to do with learning a skill.

having a tailor, a carpenter, or a mechanic in the family may mean considerable future savings well worth the apprenticeship investment, since practically all families will sooner or later need services provided by these professions.

Sending a child into apprenticeship has its costs, in terms of both the lost income from the child's labor and the price paid to the instructor, so it is not within the reach of all families. At least in theory, a child can earn the right to a "sponsored" apprenticeship. Young maids, for example, are often promised a tailoring apprenticeship if they work well and please their employer. Like any other form of payment that is withheld until an agreed service period is over, this promise serves to ensure that the girls work hard and stay obedient, and acts as a strong disincentive against running away or simply looking for another job. Sadly, apprenticeship as a reward for child labor is a promise made only slightly more often than it is broken.

While low school quality and irrelevant curricula may sometimes make apprenticeship a better investment than formal schooling, the reverse may also be true. Apprenticeship may turn out to be a way to exploit children with the excuse of teaching them valuable skills, or may simply teach poor skills because the teachers themselves do not know any better. With a fairly long time horizon (up to five years), instructors often see no reason to rush into intense technical training and may for a long time use the apprentices to run errands and do the dirty work. For example, many child apprentices also carry out common household chores in their master's workplace and even household. And, as mentioned previously, boys who are apprentices in male-only workplaces perform typically female functions, such as fetching water or preparing meals, regardless of the relevance of these tasks to the trade they are supposed to learn.

In the end, what the child will get out of the apprenticeship hinges mainly on three factors. One is the quality of the instructor: Is he or she skilled and well organized, is he or she a good instructor, is he or she fair and considerate? Another is the nature of the apprenticeship contract: Have the child's parents negotiated a clear deal or just dumped the child with the promise of paying more at a later date? The two factors, of course, are interrelated because parents who are willing and able to negotiate a clear deal will also be more likely to seek out a highly skilled tutor with a good reputation. Finally, the child's own ambition, ability, motivation, and resilience will count.

Garages

"Europe really should be paying an environment tax to Africa for dumping their old car wrecks here," laments our friend Adama, an NGO manager, as he points to a numbers of discarded old cars laying on the other side of the road from our mango tree. "Rust, old batteries, and remains of oil and gas pollute the soil, and there are so many of them!" Unknown to many Europeans, their old cars often end up in Africa. Every day, cargo ships with old cars—many of them plain wrecks—are unloaded in the main African harbors, where local businessmen take over and bring them to the nearby secondhand car markets. Some of the buyers are mechanics who see an opportunity to repair the cars and make some profit from reselling them. Others are regular buyers who within a short time will be needing the same car mechanics to start on the endless process of repairs until the car will be given up, stripped of all remaining valuable parts, and left to rust along some road.

The combination of discarded cars on the one hand, and the climate and terrible state of the roads on the other, nourishes a massive industry of local car mechanics and their garages. An African garage is normally not a solid building where cars are brought inside. Most car mechanics in Africa run their businesses from their own yard, or from a shack along a main road. To become a car mechanic is the dream of many poor African boys in both rural and urban areas. Mechanic services are in high demand everywhere. They also provide for a reasonably stable income and a certain status, particularly in rural areas, where the main alternative is farming. For many African boys, therefore, getting an apprenticeship in a garage is probably the top educational priority and preferred over formal schooling.

Remi is 10 years old and works as an apprentice with a car mechanic. The garage is not big, but still it has eight apprentices. Remi and the other young apprentices look healthy, but they are small for their age. He says: "I have been an apprentice for four years now. It was my father who decided that I should learn this work. I do not know how much he pays the mechanic. When I started working here the first days were very very difficult. I didn't know the 'mechanic language' and every time I was asked to bring a key or a tool my tutor would say, for instance, 'key for the engine, key number 14, 12.' I would always bring the wrong one and then they hit my head." When I (Anne) asked Remi how many times a day they hit his head, he said, "You don't want to know," and I realized that he didn't know, because he couldn't count. "They always send me to buy things, like food for the elders in the garage. One day they sent me to buy food and I lost the money. I cried for hours before going back to the garage, I was so afraid. When I got there the older apprentice, who runs the store when the master is not there, beat me up. Then they sent me home to get money from my father. I went back the next morning with the money. Then they beat me again because I did not come back the same day." Today he feels better because he knows his job, and he is not being punished that much. So what does Remi want to do in the future? "When I grow up I want to have a very big garage, apprentices, and make a lot of money." Will he treat his apprentices the same way he's been treated? Remi looks baffled, then says, "Yes, because that's the way they'll learn."

*   *   *

When studying the children working in garages in Tanzania, the ILO found that most of the boys were between 14 and 17 years old.[2] But even a quick look at garages in West Africa will reveal that many boys are far younger. The ILO points out that the nature of some tasks demands physical strength, like tuning up and overhauling engines, pushing broken cars, and moving heavy car parts like batteries. It is far from unusual, however, to see an oily young boy carrying a car battery in the heat of the day, probably on his way to or from a broken car or a supplier to the garage.

Injuries are common in garages, where young and inexperienced children are left in charge of adult equipment such as welding instruments. Toxic substances like gasoline and paint stripper are also in use, and inhalation can be harmful both to the nervous system and to future fertility. Burns from hot engines and welding are common. In addition, some boys are made to sleep in the garages, thus serving as night guards, with the obvious discomforts and risks involved.

Tailoring

When Price is not sitting under the mango tree with us, she tends to be sitting at an old, manually operated Singer sewing machine. But not today. Price is an apprentice with a seamstress and earlier this week she made a mistake when cutting an expensive fabric. Like in the case of Remi, her tutor has demanded that she pay for the fabric before she can continue her apprenticeship, but she has not figured out quite how to raise the money yet.

Price is especially because she had just recently been allowed to start sewing for real. Finally. She had been longing for this moment ever since she dropped out of school and came to stay in the town with her mother's cousins. The sewing machine is the heart of tailoring, and learning how to use it is the most important skill a tailor apprentice can obtain. During her first year, she was barely allowed to touch a sewing machine, but she watched very closely when older apprentices slowly turned the side wheel to start the machine and then furiously ran the fabric through, holding it with both hands. During the second year, she learned how to take measurements and use scissors, carefully cutting along the lines penciled in by her tutor. For Price, having come straight from the countryside, handling a pair of scissors accurately is actually more difficult than one might first think. So right now she is worried. Another girl at the workshop who had been unable to pay for her mis-

A tailor apprenticeship is often a reward for favored child domestic servants, and is the dream of many young school dropouts.

takes is back in her village, married to an illiterate, and working in the fields.

But Price is also worried about another thing. One of the other apprentices, Angie, has been there forever, it seems. She is now certainly beyond the age of an apprentice, but the tutor refuses to let her go, always coming up with some reason why her apprenticeship is not complete yet and why she needs to stay on. At least Angie is paid a salary, but it's very small, so who knows how long it will take her to buy her own sewing machine and set up her own business. Price's aunt told her she would stay for four years, but the tutor says that she does not know when Price will be able to graduate. The apprenticeship arrangement is relatively informal, since the tutor is a relative, so in practice Price may also end up staying several more years, like Angie.

*   *   *

Girls in Africa, like elsewhere, have an eye for fashion and beauty, and tailoring is therefore an attractive career path. African countries have their own fashion, and many are completely uninterested in Western trends. Everything from fabrics to designs follows local fashion trends, and prices fall quickly when a fabric goes out of style. A nice new outfit is more than a show of wealth. It represents a vital sign of dignity that may be particularly important to the poor, who depend more than others on social approval and therefore on being socially acceptable. And this explains why even relatively poor women often have a large selection of dresses.

To celebrate an important event such as a wedding, an anniversary, a funeral, a commemoration, or a graduation, it is not unusual that all celebrants are required to wear outfits made of a certain fabric selected for the occasion. In West Africa, groups of singing and dancing girls, all dressed identically, are a common sight at certain times of the year: they are apprentices celebrating their "liberation," the end of the apprenticeship. Similarly, after the Pope visited Malawi several years ago, his face could be seen all over the country on women's dresses, as special fabric had been made to mark the occasion. Needless to say, all this requires an army of tailors.

The older generation of tailors represents a respected profession, educated in a time when formal schooling was not common. Today's tailor apprentices instead tend to be girls who have dropped out of school, or who were never enrolled in the first place. Many come from the countryside and live with better-off urban relatives who agree to host them in exchange for help around the house—with the expectation of free tailoring services later on, perhaps. A good tailor will often have up to a dozen apprentices at the same time, at various skill levels. At the beginning, girls will run errands and do house chores. The training they receive is learned by doing, and especially by watching—apprentices are expected to be curious and attentive, but not to ask questions.[3]

Working as a tailor can be intense, often with long and late working hours. The accuracy demanded and the work position can strain eyes, neck, shoulders, and back. As a result, there are many apprentice dropouts, those who labor for months for free without any marketable skills to show for their work. Even among the good learners, many will continue assisting their tutors for years, as the salary is low and it may be difficult to save enough to actually buy a sewing machine and start up a proper business. Without a sewing machine, one cannot be a tailor.

Even used sewing machines are expensive, and without a salary, where is one supposed to find the money?

Fishing

Africa has a long coast and many lakes with abundant fishery resources, so fishing is one of the main occupations in many communities. It is not an easy job, though, as it requires strength and endurance, with rough seas and forceful currents representing constant dangers. Fishing accidents are quite common and have taken many lives—in part because, ironically, many fishermen do not know how to swim. Perhaps because of its relatively dangerous nature, it is considered a male occupation and therefore the children involved in actual fishing are almost exclusively boys. But there are also many less risky support functions surrounding the business, which are often carried out by children of both genders— cleaning and filleting the daily catch to get it ready for the market, salting and drying fish products for long-term conservation, as well as carrying nets, products, and equipment back and forth to the village.[4]

Fishermen are often poor and have only limited possibilities to send their children to school. Many families in fishing villages therefore place their children into apprenticeship, either with their own relatives or with a boat owner in the village. Since the parents are generally too poor to pay some sort of tuition and the children do perform valuable work even when they start, fishermen normally don't demand to be paid. And since the children's work is often considered to impart essential skills, they are generally not paid for their efforts. From time to time, however, especially if the day's catch is abundant, the young apprentices may be given some fish to sell for their own profit.

Fishermen's lives tend to be hard, with long hours spent on the water, grueling schedules, uncertain incomes, and frequent exposure to dangers. It would be unreasonable, therefore, to expect fishing apprentices to have it easy. In some cases, the circumstances of apprenticeship resemble slavery more than actual training, since the children work hard without a salary and have few other places to go. Representatives from Free the Slaves, a US-based NGO, discovered such extreme conditions in the fishing communities around Lake Volta, in Ghana.[5] In the Yeji fishing area, several boat owners had taken boys from the inland into apprenticelike arrangements. The boys were being prevented from leaving and used as slavelike labor. The NGO report describes the situation of three boys as follows:

The children do not receive any pay from their master but they do receive food two times a day and the children said it is usually enough. Their diet consists of, for example, kenkey (fermented corn), banku (fermented corn) or gari (cassava flour). As well, sometimes when the children are hungry in the afternoon, the master will buy them some more food. However, their hunger is by no means always satisfied. For example, Theko mentioned that the last time they had gone fishing, they were very hungry so they ate a few small fish which they had caught and the master subsequently beat them. The children sleep in a room with their master and four other boys who also work for the master. But the children's sleeping hours are short as they work through the night, perhaps with a few hours of sleep, and sometimes sleep in the afternoon.

The children all stated that the work was very difficult, especially Kwodjo who dives as well as fishes, because he is so strong. As well, the children claimed that their master beats them, sometimes with a cane and does not help them when they are hurt. Kwodjo's nails—black and broken—are evidence of this. All three boys clearly expressed their desire to return home, attend school and leave this work, which they dislike, behind.[6]

The most striking feature of this story may be that the fishermen who were mercilessly exploiting these would-be apprentices had sent their own children to school, possibly because the fish resources were about to become depleted, leaving no hope for a prosperous future.

Construction

Construction sites attract child labor in both urban and rural areas, often because they offer work that pays in cash—always a much sought-after characteristic of any employment—and because the variety of tasks to be performed makes it relatively easy to find something useful for children to do. Child labor migrants who initially came to work on farms in Côte d'Ivoire are increasingly found on construction sites after their first farming season, possibly because they have invested their earnings in an apprenticeship, or simply because after one season they have become street-wise and adventurous, and have managed to find more attractive employment in more urban areas.[7]

Children may be working on construction sites in a variety of capacities. On the one hand, there is the responsible training of mason apprentices; on the other, the use of street children and other poor children as day laborers. In between is a wide spectrum of arrangements, including the use of apprentices as free labor to carry out the most menial tasks, or the teaching of masonry skills to children employed as day laborers. The ILO's International Program for the Eradication of Child Labor has put a special focus on the construction business, because construction sites are considered risky workplaces. Transporting bricks and equipment, a task typically assigned to children, is physically demanding and may result in back and other injuries. In addition, children who work in urban construction frequently work at dangerous heights without any kind of protection. There are also risks involved with electrical installations and with some of the electrical machinery used at the larger and more sophisticated sites.

Talibés

> From the early morning, Samba Diallo improvised educational lita-nies, repeated by his companions, at the closed door of his cousin, the chief of Diallobe. The disciples [talibés] circulated this way from door to door, until they had gathered enough leftovers to nourish them through the day. Tomorrow the same search would start over again, since the disciples, who search God, did not know other life than the one of the beggar, regardless of the wealth of their parents. The door of the Chief finally opened. One of his daughters came out and gave a coin to Samba Diallo. The face of the boy remained closed. The girl placed on the ground a large plate with the leftovers from the meal from the day before. The disciples gathered around the remains and started their first meal of the day. When they had satisfied their hunger, they carefully put the rest in their cans.[8]

We have discussed some of the cultural virtues assigned to child labor in Africa. Many are convinced that hardship makes children strong, and that doing things for children, or taking care of them in an excessive manner, will harm their character development. Just as the Bible attributes virtue to sufferance and encourages parents to show their love through discipline, Islam has a similar philosophy, expressed in a striking way through the life conditions of the talibés, also known as "gari-bous," "almasiri," "almudos," or simply "the children who beg for the quranic schoolteacher."

Talibé is Arabic for "student." In West Africa, however, the word has recently gained a new meaning. It is used to describe young boys who are put in the care of quranic masters for religious studies and vir-tuous upbringing. The talibé is thus a rather special case of apprentice-ship, and a figure subject to some controversy. In our work with Muslim communities, we have found an ideological separation between what are referred to as "modern" and "ancient" quranic schools.[9] More "modern" West African Islamists forcefully reject the talibé system and the way it

The ILO is concerned about the many young boys who work at construction sites. The work is physically demanding and there are many injuries. Apprentices often work side by side with children who are day workers and are usually treated and trained better.

is practiced by more traditional quranic school masters. In a public meeting in Benin's largest Muslim city, Parakou, representatives of the modern quranic school bluntly referred to their colleagues from the "ancient" school as "slave drivers." UNICEF has defined the talibés as one of the four categories of most vulnerable children in West Africa, and in a regional report they suggest that there may be as many talibés as there are child domestic servants in the area.[10]

Easily recognizable by the empty tomato cans in which they collect leftovers to eat, the talibés are among the most visible groups of miserable children in Muslim cities, dressed in rags, hungry, and often sick.[11] They are particularly visible during the celebration of Eid and during the dry season, when rural marabous (quranic teachers) take their disciples

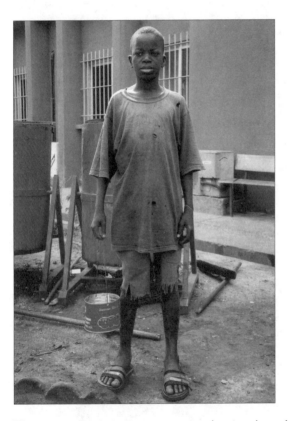

The tomato can is in many countries the sign that a begging child is a talibé, a boy placed under the tutelage of a local quranic teacher. Quranic teachers often have too many children to feed; besides, begging is deemed a worthy pursuit in itself, since it teaches the child humbleness.

to the cities to beg. The begging has two main religious functions. One is to collect the zakat, a tax that Muslims are required to pay to their religious leaders. The other is to make the talibés humble, a virtue of spiritual significance. The hunger and humiliation, alongside physical and verbal disciplining, are indeed intended to benefit the talibé children. As one marabou said to us, "It is the conscious choice of an unhappy childhood" made by parents for their sons.

The life of the talibés is beautifully illustrated by Senegalese author Cheikh Hamidou Kane in his award-winning novel about a talented talibé boy. The book is read throughout West Africa and describes the suffering of Samba Diallo, a boy who is tormented throughout his quranic schooling by his ambitious master. Is his master evil? Not at all. The master is fascinated—and also intimidated—by the extraordinary intelligence of this special boy, and through iron-fisted discipline is doing what he can to help Samba develop his potential. A typical scene from Samba's life reads:

> The smouldering log scorched his skin. The burn made him jump up, frantically shaking his light shirt. Then he sat down, cross-legged, his eyes lowered on his chalkboard, a few steps away from the master. Starting over the verse, he corrected his mistake.
>
> "Here, come close! [says his master] As long as vain thoughts will distract you from the Word, I will burn you. . . . Pay attention: you can do it. Repeat after me: 'God, give me . . .'"
>
> "God, give me attention . . ."
>
> "Again . . ."
>
> "God, give me attention . . ."
>
> "Now start your verse over."
>
> The child, shaking and submissive, started again the passionate litany of the burning verse. He repeated it until he was almost unconscious.[12]

While the talibés are mainly known for their begging, it is less known that they also do many other types of work, and most notably they often work on the farms of rural quranic teachers. We have been told that marabous rent their talibé children to commercial producers during the cotton harvest in both Benin and Burkina Faso. In Burkina, the ILO reports that child traffickers have even posed as fake marabous in order to lure parents to give away their children. Also, Malian marabous take their disciples with them to farm in Côte d'Ivoire.[13] In some towns, talibés also work as porters in markets and car stations and perform various petty services, alongside street children. In fact, in many cases it may be difficult to tell the difference between street children and talibés, as pointed out by Paul Hunt in his essay on Gambian talibés (known as almudos).[14] Street children sometimes sleep secretly in the compound of marabous who live close to markets and car stations, sneaking in after dark to find protection from the dangers of the street.[15] At times they follow their talibé friends to farm for the quranic teachers, and we found several cases of street children who had gradually become students of the Quran. But there is also a flow the other way around. After a while, urban talibés may stay permanently in the streets where they work and live, while rural talibés sometimes remain in the streets of the city when their master goes back to the village after Eid.

4

Child Labor in the Commercial Labor Market

THE GENERAL UNDEREMPLOYMENT IN AFRICA GIVES EMPLOYERS A strong bargaining power, as people are often willing to work even for very low and uncertain salaries. When some commercial employers choose to employ children, it is normally in order to press the rates even lower, because the nature of the work is such that adults would rather not take it. As Africa is largely unindustrialized, relatively few workplaces employ high numbers of workers, with the possible exception of some sectors of commercial agriculture and certain mining companies. Both mining and commercial agriculture are often based on leasing land, subcontracting of production, and tenant systems, so that work tends to be carried out in small, informal workplaces. As a result, public labor market regulations are applicable in only a few cases, and the monitoring and enforcement of child labor laws in most cases become extremely difficult.

Child labor performed in the commercial labor market tends to have little educational value. When children enter this market, they generally have one immediate objective: to make money. As a result, it is not unusual for them to change jobs frequently as they pursue better earnings. The purpose for working may differ depending on the family situation and the child's personality. It may be to support their siblings, to take care of their own basic needs, or to buy a coveted "luxury item" like a radio. Thus there may be child street vendors who are desperately trying to help out their parents, side by side with those who work to cover their school fees and those who work to buy themselves a radio or a bicycle. To illustrate the frequency with which children may change

The main objective for children who work in the commercial labor market is to make money—not to learn. Many children also run their own businesses, like this boy, who has his own little selection of merchandise to sell in a car station.

jobs looking for better opportunities, the introductory quotations to all sections of this chapter are taken from a Somali girl named Aman. All the events she describes took place when she was between seven and eight years old.[1]

*   *   *

African households tend to have highly unstable incomes and very little savings. Not only is there seldom enough to spare, but whatever is miraculously saved is often shared with the less fortunate members of the extended family. This solidarity among family members is an essential feature of African life, because it is a very effective safety net in moments of crisis—most times, it is the only safety net there is. The downside to this practice is that African communities have little to fall back on when a large share of the population is hit at once—for example, in the case of natural disasters or epidemics. However, as long as each family follows its own individual rhythm of ups and downs, this mutuality system helps smooth income variability, and at the same time makes the family stronger and the community more united, thereby contributing to development of social capital. If the family and community support mechanisms are reasonably functional, a household in trouble will receive enough support to be able to get back on its feet. With an amazing ingenuity, African families time and again pull themselves out of a crisis and manage to make a new start, often in a new business.

All family members pitch in during a downturn, and children are no exception. Therefore, many children work off and on, and abandon and reenter school, depending on the fortunes of their families. Although some children are taken out of school because of mediocre teachers or achievement, many of the dropout rates can be explained by a temporary income need in a child's family. Typical occasions can be to help pay for an expensive funeral, to make up for the lost salary of a sick or deceased relative, to repay a debt, or to rebuild or improve a damaged house. Some households are more or less permanently in a crisis, leaving the children more or less permanently in the labor market, but in many cases children work only after school hours, during school holidays, or for a limited period during a temporary hardship. When the family economy is restored, the children often—but unfortunately not always—go back to their more ordinary activities in school or in the household.

Outside crises, children generally try to combine school and work, but sometimes the opportunity of taking a good job simply cannot be missed, and considerations about convenient timing are given less priority. A good example is road construction. Children from the area around the construction site often drop out of school temporarily to do construction work or to provide support services for adult workers. Harvest time is another example, and in the places where school holidays are not adjusted to the most labor-intensive agricultural seasons, many children will abandon school periodically to participate in the harvesting.

Commercial Agriculture

I heard that jobs were opening up in a new agricultural project, and they were hiring a lot of people. So I went back to my relative, the District Commissioner, and told him I wanted a job. He told me I was too young for that job—it was a fifteen-mile walk outside the village,

morning and evening, thirty miles each day. He said it would be too
hard for me, but I said, "Never mind. I want it. I can do it." So he talked
to somebody who sent word to me to come to work. And I went to work.[2]

The ILO estimates that about 20 percent of the people working in commercial agriculture in Africa are children. Most of them, however, do not work full time because they combine school and work. Therefore, some children work full days but only during school holidays, and others work half days while going to school. Some large plantations even have their own schools for the children who live and work on the estate. The workload, however, leads to high dropout rates, as reported from Tanzania.[3]

Commercial farming in Africa encompasses a multitude of cash crops ranging from cowpeas and manioc sold on domestic markets, to tobacco and coffee grown for export. With the exception of a handful of countries with a considerable production of highly prized minerals like oil (Nigeria, Gabon, Equatorial Guinea) and diamonds (Botswana, Sierra Leone), the main income from African exports comes from agriculture. Among the most important export crops are cocoa, coffee, tea, tobacco, rice, fruits, sugar, groundnuts, rubber, and cotton. The majority of countries concentrate heavily on one or two crops (e.g., coffee accounts for 80 percent of Burundi's exports and cotton for 80 percent of Benin's), and relatively few have a diverse agricultural export sector.

The extent to which children participate in commercial farming depends above all on the type of crop. Certain crops are more demanding of the type of labor that children can provide, while others provide few or no tasks that children could perform. Cotton and coffee plantations, for example, can employ large numbers of children as pickers at harvest time, while chopping sugar cane or cutting down cocoa fruits requires greater strength and is therefore generally done by strong adolescents or adult men. Although harvesting may not always be suitable for children, weeding is definitely considered appropriate child work. This may be because it requires relatively little supervision. However, since it involves bending and crawling, and is done almost exclusively by women and children, we can also assume that it has a fairly low status. Children are found weeding all sorts of crops.

Children's involvement in commercial farming also depends on the production system. Studies carried out under the ILO's International Program for the Eradication of Child Labor found that in Kenya, the number of children working on sugar farms owned by individual farmers or subcontractors was higher than the number working

Children working for commercial producers are often underpaid, but the cash income is welcomed by both the children and their families. Cotton picking is a common child labor task, since it is relatively easy and children have the right height to pick from the lower branches.

on company-owned plantations. On the other hand, company-owned coffee plantations employed more children than did individually owned estates.[4]

Commercial farmers employ children either as individual workers or as part of a "family package." In the first case, children tend to be grossly underpaid—half, a third, or even less of a man's salary, even for the same work. Employers may claim that children are slower or that their work is of lesser quality, but in many cases they are honest enough to admit that the main reason is simply that they can get away with paying less—which is frequently the case, especially if the children are alone and away from home. When kids are employed as part of a "family package," they are normally not paid at all, as payment tends to be based on quantities produced or harvested. In Malawi, children of tobacco tenants share the family burden as adjustable labor in periods of intensive farming, either by helping to fill the family quotas or by filling in for their parents when they have to perform other estate work. In her book *The Smoking Business,* Liv Tørres writes:

> It is not by accident or choice that children get involved in the production of tobacco. The system is designed so that the tenants have no

choice but to involve the entire family in the production of tobacco. Indeed, tenants are recruited on the basis that they have a family, which they will bring to the estate to work. . . . Children are usually not employed directly on the estates but work as part of the tenant family. When a tenant is employed on the estate he or she is employed as head of the household and is responsible for fulfilling the quota required by the estate owner. This quota cannot be grown unless the entire family of the tenant is involved in tobacco growing.[5]

It is becoming more difficult to investigate child labor on large estates and plantations because estate owners and managers, increasingly aware of legal regulations, are not keen on letting researchers snoop around. On the other hand, commercial plantations may be the one type of workplace in Africa where international conventions and national laws on children's rights could indeed prove to be efficient tools in reducing child labor. In fact, large estates are much easier to monitor than are the many small farms of subcontractors, while family-controlled child labor on parental farms will need a whole different range of social interventions in order to be reduced.

Child Domestic Services

I told Habib's wife, "Yes, I want to go to work for them." . . . The next Friday we met the family, and they told me they were going to treat me like their daughter. . . . The first night the woman made me sleep on the floor, on a thin little mat. I couldn't sleep because the floor was so cold. . . . I wouldn't have minded if it had been a dirt floor, but it was cement. I had never slept on cement before in all my life. . . . And I became sick with coughing, a cold, and fever. The woman made me work like a big person, although I wasn't even eight years old yet. She made me work hard, hard, until I washed the last glass, the last spoon. Ah! Sweep the house, mop, make the bed—work like I was a big person. Sometimes I could not wash the clothes—when they got wet, they were heavy, and I could not lift them, so I just stirred them with my hand. When I became sick, she didn't do anything about it. At night, when I was cold, I would cough and sneeze, and my body would have chills, and then be hot as fire. The next morning I had to wake up and work. Even if she just wanted water in the middle of the night, she would wake me up and make me get it. She wasn't feeding me right. I was hungry all the time because she would only give me leftovers. . . . I had to wait until they finished. Then, to what was left over on their plate, she would add one or two more spoonfuls, and bring me the dirty plate they had eaten on. . . . I still

The duty of child domestics is to cover the needs of everybody else. Their own needs are often completely neglected. This tends to lead to an underdeveloped self-identity.

dream that I'm always hungry and she is scolding me about the cough and saying, Never do that again.[6]

Domestic service is probably the largest commercial market for children's labor in Africa, but because of the hidden nature of this type of work, it is difficult to estimate how many children (mostly girls) are employed as house servants. Not all girls who live with nonrelatives can be assumed to be servants, while some girls are treated as servants even by close relatives. To obtain a rough estimate for Lomé, Togo's capital, officials in the Directorate of Employment and Labor calculated that all civil servants of a certain level and above would have at least one servant girl, and that well-off traders would also have domestic help, producing an estimate of 50,000 young household helpers (only expatriates and the very rich would have adult servants). Similarly, a focused study found that one in three families in Lomé had at least one servant girl.[7] If the latter is representative of urban areas in Africa in general, and assuming an average household size of five, the number of child domestic servants in Africa would approximate 14 million.[8]

Child domestic servants are easy to acquire for urban households in most of Africa, since there are plenty of destitute girls, and many rural parents consider child "placement" in urban areas as an opportunity for the child and an income source for the family. Children are also cheap to hire. With poor negotiating skills and almost no bargaining power, they end up being paid very meager salaries (of the order of 30–40¢ a day) or no salary at all (just board and lodging), making them affordable even to average urban earners. Ironically, the exploitation of child domestic servants is frequently pictured as a charitable act by the employer—taking in a poor rural girl who would otherwise face a life of hardship in the village. This further blurs the distinction between child fostering and child domestic employment. In practice, fostering and domestic service are better understood as opposite ends of a continuum, with most urban living arrangements for rural children having elements of both.

The nature and the stage of evolution of child domestic service vary among African countries. While in Burkina Faso the line between child fostering and domestic service tends to be extremely fuzzy in most cases, child domestics in Senegal may live outside the household and cater to several families—just as cleaning women do in industrialized countries. In Dakar, groups of rural child migrants often share the rent for the room they live in, and it is not unusual to find older child domestics training younger ones. In Kenya, child domestics are likely to change employers more often than is typical in West Africa. A suggested reason is that the woman of the house will attempt to replace her young maids frequently in order to prevent her husband from getting too closely involved with one particular girl. Her fear is legitimate, since it is not uncommon for men to throw out their wives and replace them with the maids. Although jealousy certainly is a factor also in West African households, the common practice of polygamy somewhat reduces the risk faced by the wife.

Child domestic service is harmful, mentally perhaps even more than physically, and often has long-term negative consequences for the child servant. Child domestics tend to grow up in an environment where their sole value is their ability to satisfy the needs of others, and where their own needs, let alone their preferences, matter to nobody. In her research and action handbook on child domestic workers, Maggie Black distinguishes between their *disadvantages* and their *indignities:*

"Disadvantages could include such things as eating leftovers, having no personal space or bed, working very long hours, and isolation. The word indignities implies something else: damage to one's sense of self, and to one's existence as free independent and equal human being." On the last point, she stresses the negative consequences of "being regarded as a creature with no individual will or viewpoints whose quality of existence is entirely at the mercy of the employers' family."[9]

Aman, the Somali girl quoted at the start of this section, was lucky. When her proud mother came to visit her, she almost broke the employer's neck and immediately took her daughter back home. Odile, who is pictured in Chapter 6, was also treated badly, but when her father went to get her, the employer refused to let her go. A humble peasant, the father returned to the village without his daughter. These cases, however, are exceptions. Generally, poor rural parents have little chance to maintain contact with their children who have gone to the city, and the harshness of their own daily life may make them turn a blind eye even when they suspect that their child is suffering. This attitude is also excused by the argument that hardship is good for children and that learning to work hard will help them later in life. We have interviewed children who had run away from extremely abusive employers, only to be reprimanded and brought back to their employers by their own parents.

Young maids tend to be dismissed around the age of 15, when they become more difficult to control. They also become vulnerable to the sexual interest of men in the household, and more aware of this fact themselves. Once dismissed, former child domestics face an uncertain future. They often cannot—or will not—return to their village, and in any case they are not trained to farm. With little or no schooling, few marketable skills, and a weak solidarity network, they become less

In the opening chapter of his book *Disposable People,* Kevin Bales interviews a young Malian woman, age 22, who has spent her entire life as a domestic servant under extreme conditions. Until she was liberated she had little understanding of time, with no knowledge of weeks, months, or years. She knew that there were hot seasons and cold seasons, but she never learned that the seasons followed a pattern. Bales asked her to draw a man as best that she could, and this is the result.

attractive to employers as domestic servants and few options remain open. Their vulnerability makes them easy prey for the next exploiter in line, be it a boyfriend, a husband, an employer, or a pimp. This last possibility is not an exaggeration. Interviews with prostitutes in Nairobi and Cotonou revealed that the majority of them shared a similar story: Some had been sent into domestic service as young as 3, most had been sexually abused at an early age, and many had been sexually abused by a member of the employer's household.[10]

Petty Trade

> When you are a bread-seller, you go to the bakery with your bag and your cloth and give the baker the money for the bread and then wrap the hot, freshly-baked bread up in the cloth and put it in the bag, and then you go out and start selling. You call out "Bread! Bread! Bread for sale!" And people come out of their houses and buy as much as they want.[11]

Small commerce is a very common activity for women in Africa.[12] They may sell directly from their houses, go door to door, set up makeshift stalls in the street (often just a piece of cloth or a large basket on the ground), or walk the streets with their merchandise on their head. Typically, everybody in the neighborhood knows who has ice, oil, cooked food, or bread, and at what price. Other women may send a child or a domestic servant to buy the merchandise, or use the opportunity themselves to catch up on the latest neighborhood news.

Even the most unobservant visitor to an African market cannot help but notice that next to the women traders are children, either helping out or doing their own business. Children, and especially girls, are often expected to contribute to their mother's business.[13] If they go to school, they frequently spend their lunch break helping their mothers sell home-cooked food in crowded areas—near markets, offices, factories, ports, and stations. If they don't go to school, petty trade may be their full-time occupation, particularly in urban areas. While this type of activity is largely harmless, there are risks involved, particularly for girls who sell in secluded, male-dominated workplaces or who go door-to-door, often entering people's compounds. It is not unusual for children who sell food in car stations to be harassed by drivers, and most girls selling door-to-door have at some stage experienced sexual advances from men who were alone at home. We interviewed Mary, an 11-year-old sales girl who had been robbed by a prospective client and then locked in a room. The second night, Mary managed to escape, but did not dare to return to the woman for whom she sold, fearing that she would be accused of having stolen the money herself.

Child domestic servants are frequently used as street vendors for the employer's family business, making them an income source for their employers and sometimes even net contributors to the household. This helps explain why the poorest 20 percent of urban households in Benin were found to be just as likely to have foster children as were middle-income families.[14] From the children's point of view, being sent out to peddle merchandise has the advantage of breaking their isolation and giving them some experience with sales. In a Nigerian study, it was pointed out how child vendors learned to woo costumers to induce impulsive buying, to distinguish bona fide costumers from fraudulent or criminal ones, to elbow other sellers away in competitive situations, to compute quickly and give the correct change, and to do simple accounting without using paper. These abilities are not only beneficial for cognitive development, but also useful survival skills.[15] On the other hand, the young vendors are often put under a lot of pressure to bring money home, and may be punished if they fail to meet a daily quota. Besides, spending long hours in the streets exposes them to pollution, accidents, and harassment—from adults, street children, and even the police.

Some businesses go as far as speculating by taking in several children for business purposes. Such enterprises tend to be highly abusive, as in the testimony of a Ghanian social worker:

I knew a woman at Katamanto Market. She had about 12 girls between the ages of 9 and 13. All the girls had to go out every day to sell ice water. They got a gallon of water, and the woman knew how many cups they would sell. When the girls came back, they were supposed to bring 350 cedis [about 20¢ at that time, mid-1999]. If they brought back less, they were beaten. . . . the woman promised the girls that if they stayed with her for two years, she would buy them a sewing machine. And if they stayed for longer than that she would get them training. But I never saw the woman buying a machine for the girls. Something always happened before the two years were up, and the woman would sack the girl. I constantly saw new girls coming to stay with this woman.[16]

Work as a Porter

[My little brother] Hassan began to work too—he would go to the market with Mama in the morning and carry things for people, so he was bringing home a little money.[17]

The majority of children employed in cash crop production and petty commerce work with their own family or guardians, but there are also many self-employed children in the commercial labor market. Even children as young as 7 may have their own small trade businesses, typically buying petty commodities (candy, chewing-gum, peanuts) and reselling them in the streets and in markets. For those who cannot afford to invest in basic products for reselling, the last resort tends to be working as porters in markets and stations.

Working as a porter is about as low as one can go in African societies. The loads are heavy, the fees small, and the incomes unreliable. Carrying for others is also regarded as a low-status work, so its market value is partly derived from the prestige attached to employing someone else to carry for you. It is generally a job of last resort, as it requires nothing but muscles, endurance, and a willingness to sweat. When no salaried employment can be found and not even a tiny amount of money to start a petty trade is available, hiring out oneself as a porter is one of the few legal options left. For this reason, it is often an activity for children in crisis, and common for talibés (boys begging for quranic teachers) and street children.

A study on girls in difficult situations in Lomé described how those who find themselves on their own often end up as coltineuses, that is, porters.[18] They transport the merchandise of traders from bus terminals to the market or from a warehouse to sale points, carry heavy parcels to the buyer's means of transport, and often also help unload trucks. The girls go to the market or the bus stations early in the morning and only stop at about six or seven o'clock in the evening. Lunch is generally skipped to save money and to maximize the time spent working. They work barefoot so they can walk faster. Incomes vary greatly depending on the luck of the day, but on average, daily earnings could be the equivalent of about a dollar. Coltineuses tend to sleep in parking lots or bus stations near the main market in groups of forty to sixty, paying the equivalent of 5–10¢ per night for protection; many of them complain that, despite the money paid to a guard, they feel unsafe, and rapes are not uncommon.

The work of coltineuses in Lomé is fairly typical. In most African markets, children hang around and wait for people to shop for more than they can—or are willing to—carry. In some markets, children are able to rent pushcarts, so that alone or with the help of a friend they can transport an even bigger load. Child porters are also often found in car stations and other places where travelers are expected to need help with their luggage. Adult men can be found working as porters in stations and ports but rarely in markets, possibly because markets are the sphere of women and stations the hangout of drivers and mechanics. It is also possible that travelers have more money and pay better for porter services than do women shopping in the markets. Kwame, a 10-year-old porter boy in Takoradi, says:

Not long after I came, my father went back to the village. He's been gone for more than three weeks now, and he did not leave us anything. I'm working as a porter to feed myself and my brothers and sisters. . . . I hope my father comes back soon, because I want to save money to go back to school.[20]

In Ghana, the women and children who carry parcels in the markets go by the name of *kayayei* or *kayayoo*. *Kayayoo* are typically migrants from the countryside who work short-term to try to save up some money to start a small business, to pay for apprenticeship training, or to fund a dowry. Since *kayayoo* are often girls who have higher ambitions, they sometimes organize mutual savings groups, which tend to be restricted to girls from the same village to minimize the risk of cheating.[19] Some such groups run revolving funds, which grant each girl, in turn, the opportunity to invest in something beyond basic daily necessities.

Children who work as porters are often among the most destitute. The load of this street child in Niger would hurt the neck of anybody, but is particularly painful for a hungry and malnourished child. To other children, being a porter for a short period is a way to save the little capital that is needed in order to start up a petty trade business or to pay for an apprenticeship.

Working in Bars and Restaurants

After about three months I went back to my uncle, the District Commissioner, and told him I wanted to change jobs. There was another job, as a waitress at the big hotel—the place for government officials to stay when they were in town. The hotel was closer to my house, and it paid the same as my job in the farm project. He said, "Why not? Good idea!" I worked an eight-hour-shift. . . . The manager and everybody knew me, and all the older people liked me. . . . I had such a long way to come. I had to cross the river from the other side, and early in the morning hippos were grazing along the road sometimes, and it was dangerous. So the manager said, "Take your time. Leave the house at six-thirty and be at work at seven." That was wonderful. I said, "Thank you, Uncle."[21]

Running a bar or a small restaurant is another common business for African women. It need not be a formal setup—a bar or restaurant can be as simple as a bench with a table in front of the house, or a few plastic chairs in a compound. Hours of operation tend to be very flexible, as they basically depend on whether there are clients to serve and something to serve them, and it is not unusual to find that such a restaurant has run out of food, especially after peak hours. In general, the waitress is the daughter of the owner, one of her foster children, or a child domestic servant.

African children tend to find bar and restaurant jobs much more attractive than most other work. They bring in a regular (although often meager) income, they take place in a convivial atmosphere, and above all, such jobs are not as hard and dirty as working in the fields, which is the most common alternative. It is understandable how waiting on tables at first glance may seem appealing.

In reality, working in bars and restaurants proves to be significantly less glamorous than many children expect. Girls may have to spend long hours pounding maize or manioc. This is hard work, best compared, say, to lifting free weights for five hours straight. But the main drawback of working in bars and restaurants is that in many cases the venues provide their male clients with services that go beyond food and drinks, something that is especially the case with small-town motels. Girls may be lured or pressured into sexual involvement with clients, while others may move from restaurant to restaurant to avoid such pressures. In West Africa, many girls serving in bars and restaurants come from neighboring countries. Far from home, underpaid, working late hours in a place where alcohol is served, and constantly approached by drivers and other travelers, it is often just a question of time before they become involved in prostitution. This may or may not have been the owner's intention, but with no general responsibility for the girl and acknowledging that it is good for business, the owner is not very likely to interfere. Actually, it is not unusual for bar or motel owners to take a cut of the payment, although, when asked, they tend to present a lamenting charade on the lack of morals exhibited by their girls.

On our journeys through Africa we have stayed regularly in many such small-town motels, and we have noticed the way the young waitresses are frequently replaced by new ones. Employed on the basis of their appearance, there is little doubt that the girls are expected to be willing to provide extra services to the guests. Should they become ill or pregnant—like "Marian" in the photograph below—replacements are readily available.

We met "Marian" regularly over the several years we were working in northern Benin. At age 12 she was thrilled to get to work in a small-town motel, despite a meager income and working sixteen to seventeen hours a day, seven days a week. However, local motels often pose great risks to young girls, and at the age of 16 she finds herself pregnant—and fired.

5

The Worst Forms
of Child Labor

MANY TYPES OF WORK PERFORMED BY AFRICAN CHILDREN JEOPARDIZE their health, safety, and morals, but certain jobs do so more than most. These jobs are known as "the worst forms," in reference to the ILO's Convention 182. According to Article 3 of this convention "concerning the prohibition and immediate action for the elimination of the worst forms of child labor," the worst forms comprise:

> (a) all forms of slavery or practices similar to slavery, such as the sale and trafficking of children, debt bondage and serfdom and forced or compulsory labour, including forced or compulsory recruitment of children for use in armed conflict; (b) the use, procuring or offering of a child for prostitution, for the production of pornography or for pornographic performances; (c) the use, procuring or offering of a child for illicit activities, in particular for the production and trafficking of drugs as defined in the relevant international treaties; (d) work which, by its nature or the circumstances in which it is carried out, is likely to harm the health, safety or morals of children.

This chapter describes five of the so-called worst forms. Convention 182 explicitly mentions two of them: child soldiering and child prostitution. The other three—child quarrying, child mining, and the economic activities of street children—are included because they are considered to be particularly hazardous due to the nature of the work and the environment in which the work takes place. They would thus be organized under item (d) of Article 3 as quoted above. These five forms of child labor, however, are not really comparable.

Mining and quarrying result from perverse structures that allow for the exploitative use of poor and desperate children, while the presence of street children is often a sign of social disintegration. The use of children in prostitution and armed combat, on the other hand, is so abusive that it is questionable whether these occupations even deserve the label "labor."

All of the children working in the worst forms of child labor, however, have one thing in common. They are likely to be so hurt by their work that, if they survive, they have a very slim chance of ever becoming normally functioning citizens. The costs of trying to rehabilitate a child who has been involved in one of the worst forms are so high, and the probability of success is so limited, that the main strategy worth recommending is to do everything possible to prevent more children from ending up in such situations.

Quarries

In 1996 the ILO estimated that 0.9 percent of economically active children worldwide worked in mines and quarries.[1] In 2002 it further estimated that 66 million children in Africa were economically active.[2] If these figures are representative of African reality, about 600,000 African children are employed in such workplaces today.

The demand for gravel is high in most developing countries, as it is widely used in all types of construction. Knowing that simple machinery can easily and rapidly crush stone, it is puzzling to see how breaking rocks is still performed by hand in so many African countries. One can only assume that the salary of the people working in the quarries must be so low that it compensates for the overwhelmingly low productivity of manual labor. As we have seen, one way of keeping salaries down is to employ children, so it is no surprise that children are often found manually breaking stones to make gravel.

There are quarries all over Africa, sometimes near "regular" villages or cities and other times within their own separate quarrying communities. These communities are often populated by destitute people who have become estranged from their kin and their original homeland. In Burkina Faso, for example, there are quarries mainly inhabited by women who, after their husband's death, have run away from forced marriage to one of his brothers.[3] These women now live in the quarries with their children, who start helping their mothers basically as soon as they can hold a hammer—payment comes for the amount of gravel produced, so even clumsy little hands can make a difference. In Tanzania, having a stepparent is a much cited reason why children leave for the quarries, because it frequently happens that stepparents, and especially stepmothers, mistreat their spouse's children from previous marriages.[4] When no other family member is willing to take care of the children, going to the quarrying site is just one of the few alternatives to ending up in the streets.

Roles and hierarchies in quarrying communities are often fairly rigid. Men have two main but quite different functions. On the one hand, they drill and lay the explosives for breaking new rocks. On the other, they are responsible for relationships with buyers and negotiating sales, something that gives them financial control over the production. Women and children gather the rocks and transport them to their huts or day tents, where they finally sit down to break them into gravel of various sizes. Children also frequently work in support functions, mainly as messengers, water sellers, and food sellers. Transporting rocks is very hard work, and breaking them is tedious. In addition, injuries from tools and rock splinters are common, especially for children, who frequently hit their hands.

Stone quarries and the surrounding communities are generally places of unspeakable misery where the poorest and most vulnerable members of society try to eke out a living. Hard work, hunger, and disease are ever-present—the dust causes respiratory problems, and poor sanitary conditions cause diarrhea.[5] With survival often being the only goal, norm systems are weak and the sense of solidarity that is characteristic of African communities tends to be missing. In this context, child prostitution can become part of the survival strategy. Developing sexual relationships with adult men on the site not only provides the children with food, but can also serve as a protection strategy against other men. Due to the prostitution and strategic sexual behavior, children in some quarry sites suffer from venereal disease.

While such extreme working conditions would suggest that quarrying represents a last resort for outcasts and the landless, many children working in quarries have actually chosen this life over unpaid work in the family business or on the family farm. When interviewed, some of them claimed that they were saving money to go back to school. In reality, they seldom continue their education because they lose their initial ambition to disease and disillusion, and saving money turns out to be nearly impossible. Many also stay on simply because quarrying is their world and the only job they know.

Mines

Gold, copper, nickel, iron, coal, and uranium are found all over the African continent, and so are gemstones. Mining sites and their commu-

We were constantly hit by splinters while taking pictures in quarries in Benin and Burkina Faso, and the bodies of many of the children were covered in small sores. Their eyes, in particular, are subject to serious injury and infection.

nities in many ways resemble quarrying sites and their respective communities. The extraction process in this case, as well, is tedious and labor-demanding, but mining communities tend to be better organized and have more infrastructure. While some children are employed full time at the mining site, many are not. Some work only during school holidays, and others during the dry season, when there is no farm work. In comparison to quarrying, mining attracts many more men and boys than women and girls. Girls are for the most part employed in support activities, such as bringing the water needed to wash the sand and extract the grains of gold that may be hiding within it.

Sebastian Junger, a journalist on special assignment in Sierra Leone, described diamond mining as follows:

> [The diamond fields] are just gravel pits carved out of the jungle, dotted with teenage boys in their underwear shoveling mud. . . . The young miners were friendly, stopping their work to ask for cigarettes when we pulled over. They worked in shifts in the hammering sun, digging down into the diamond-bearing gravel and piling it up on the side to be sorted. Alluvial mining is not dramatic or dangerous or even costly; it just requires a lot of people digging. . . . The diggers are fed twice a day, paid a nominal amount of money, and given a share of whatever diamonds are found. . . . Typically, a third of the stones are turned over to the workers, a third are kept by financial backers, and a third given to the land-owner. Obviously, it is a system full of opportunities to steal someone blind.[6]

In Guinea, children as young as 14 work in diamond mines. The Ministry of Children and Family reports that these children tend to become indebted to their employer and often end up working under endless contracts to pay back loans they have taken to buy food or medicine. The starting point of this vicious circle can probably be traced back to the fact that child miners are often underpaid, partly because they have no idea of the real value of diamonds, partly because they are cheated, and partly because, as a general rule, children get a lower share of the team's compensation.[7] On the other hand, mining also has the strong appeal of cash. A teacher in Tanzania noted that "children abandon school once they get money quickly within a short period of time."[8]

Life as a miner is indeed brutal, and even more so for child miners. In mining communities, child prostitution and strategic sexual behavior are commonplace because the concentration of male workers away from their families tends to be high. Sexual abuse—of boys as well as girls—is also probably relatively common. Health officials in the mining areas of Burkina Faso, for example, report sexually transmitted diseases

The mining sector is extremely hazardous and exploitative. Children in the gold mines work without safety equipment, sometimes as deep as sixty meters underground.

among gold-mining children, a problem difficult to explain in the absence of prostitution and sexual abuse.[9] However, there is one easy way to forget the hardships, and we have personally witnessed its availability: At dawn during one of our visits to a Burkina Faso mining site, drug dealers appeared among the small mountains of excavated sand. Groups of adolescent miners started gathering to self-medicate their pain, and we were told to leave the area for the sake of our own security.

Prostitution

I arrived in the street when I was 7 years old. I had to obey the rules of the older children. . . . I knew that I could not make it on my own. I easily got friends, and in the beginning they were very nice. They taught me how to make a living, and how to escape the dangers of crooks and of ordinary people. One night, the older children woke me up and explained to me that I had to reimburse them for helping me. They started to undress me and they held me. I did not want to, but they forced me. After that I was fucked every night, until I got big enough to defend myself. When you have been fucked you have to work all day for the one who fucks you at night: clean cars, beg, hunt for food, and steal with

him. If an old or a disabled man wants your ass, he will pay your friend,
and off you go. They can make a lot of money that way. . . . The first time
you take a new kid, you are very violent, because you want to revenge
all that you have suffered. . . . Those who are initiated suffer a lot, and
there is a lot of blood.[10]

We have chosen to present the above story, told not by a girl but by a
15-year-old street boy in Senegal, for two reasons. First, we want to
break the stereotype of the girl prostitute. Second, we want to illustrate
the fact that most of the African children who have ever been paid for
sex are not full-time prostitutes, but sell sexual services from time to
time—when they are hungry, forced, or lured.

Perhaps the best way to understand the nature of child prostitution
in Africa is to start with gender relations. Women and girls are systematically discriminated against in most African societies. Men sit in most
positions of authority and, more important, tend to occupy positions that
give them access to cash. Particularly among the poor, one of the few
ways for a woman or girl to access goods and services controlled by
men is through a man. While this would preferably be a father, a son, a
husband, or a brother, some are forced or tempted to commercialize the
only good in demand that a poor girl possesses: her body. Trading sex
for access to jobs, higher education, cash, or other benefits is a logical
strategy when the playing field is far from even and opportunities are
very limited. Sometimes it is the only strategy possible. In Equatorial
Guinea, a country marked by extreme inequality and social disintegration after decades of dictatorship, occasional prostitution is a common
survival strategy. It is apparently quite normal for a woman to offer her
services when she needs cash, and also young girls can be used for this
purpose. There seems to be little stigma attached to this type of activity—it is simply seen as a commercial transaction done for a legitimate
purpose. During the summer holidays, many teenage girls, as young as
14, cross the borders with Gabon and Cameroon to find work as prostitutes. This summer job allows them to eat, buy new clothing, and come
back with some savings for their families.[11] This sort of transactional
sex is by no means a peculiarity of Equatorial Guinea or reserved to
countries in similarly dire circumstances.

While urban prostitution is most well known, rural prostitution also
exists, particularly in crisis periods such as famines and droughts. As a
farmer told us, "You know who has an empty granary when you see the
woman leaving her hut at night to visit a man." Sometimes, the one
leaving the hut at night is not a woman but a girl. There was no con-
demnation in his voice, just a bit of pity. More than anything else, there

was acceptance—people run into problems and try to solve them as best they can. If selling sex is the best a woman can do, so be it. And sometimes the reason is not an empty granary. As the AIDS epidemic has revealed, some teachers use their positions of power to sexually abuse pupils, even those in elementary school. Female students are sometimes coerced into sexually serving their teachers to cover school fees and in exchange for better grades.

The AIDS epidemic is putting a new spin on the issue of transactional sex. While some girls have always relied on "sugar daddies" to finance their secondary studies, fear of AIDS has provided many more opportunities as men look for increasingly younger sexual partners and are willing to pay for them.[12] Particularly dangerous is the belief common in some parts of Africa that having sex with a virgin will cure or

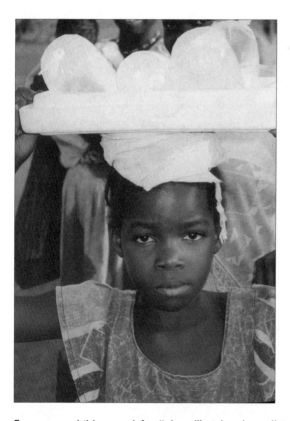

For street children and for "placed" girls who sell in car stations and other male-dominated workplaces, it is often only a question of time before lack of family follow-up, ignorance, emotional starvation, male pressure, or plain hunger drive many into occasional prostitution.

prevent AIDS. Many men will pay a high price to avoid the "slim disease," and the temptation for poor parents—and poor girls—may indeed be too much to resist, with predictable consequences. In southern Africa, 15- to 19-year-old girls have six times the HIV infection rate of boys their age. To this must be added the fact that the negotiating skills and experience of children are normally weak, and therefore children are easily taken advantage of, even when they sell sex voluntarily. The South African NGO Molo Songololo quotes a client of child prostitutes who puts it like this: "Most truck drivers prefer young girls because they charge less . . . and always consent to sex without a condom."[13]

For the much smaller share of children who engage in full-time prostitution, it is often of a different type than the occasional sex work that many vendors undertake. In a report from Tanzania it was noted that "to survive in prostitution one needs a great deal of courage and a large dose of initiative. Engaging in prostitution is not for anyone; it is for those who can cope. The children in the business have already made their own decisions and developed strategies for coping and surviving around prostitution."[14] Unfortunately, the courageous child prostitutes have a high mortality rate—from AIDS, violence, and drugs.

Child Soldiers

In 2002, as reported by the ILO, there were 120,000 child soldiers under age 18 in Africa, some as young as 7.[15] Children are found within government forces in Chad, Eritrea, and Ethiopia; within both government forces and armed opposition groups in Angola, Burundi, the Democratic Republic of Congo, Congo-Brazzaville, Rwanda, and Uganda; and within government forces, armed opposition groups, and paramilitaries in Sierra Leone, Somalia, and Sudan.[16]

The stories about child soldiers told by the media and some NGOs tend to be about the most horrific cases. For example, that of a Mozambican boy who was forced to kill his own parents and then abducted and forced to go on killing. Or that of Sierra Leonian young rebel fighters who had cocaine implanted in their arms by the commanders to make them commit atrocities without questioning their actions. We don't blame journalists or activists for wanting to tell these stories, since they may have value not only in terms of "letting the world know" but also for shocking decisionmakers into action. They are misleading, however, in that they give the impression that those horror stories are typical.

Although abductions of children by armed groups are indeed com-

This boy is currently in a rehabilitation camp for former child soldiers in Sierra Leone. The weapon he is posing with is probably of much higher quality than the arms that child soldiers are normally allowed to use. (Photo by Giacomo Piroizzi, UNICEF)

mon, not all child soldiers are abducted. Many, if not most, recruit themselves as a way out of communities and families that are disintegrating during war and time of conflict. Conflict often occurs when the social fabric is seriously weakened and certainly creates further disintegration.

War leads to displacement, refugee movements, family fragmentation, and parental loss, all factors that stimulate the self-recruitment of children looking for stability and protection. In its more benign manifestations, war has consequences also for communities that are not directly involved in conflict. For example, farmers may fear going to the fields or be unable to purchase needed inputs, which results in underemployment, crop failure, and eventually famine. In these cases, children—and perhaps older brothers—may decide to join the armed forces out of hunger and frustration. It is also true that many boys look up to armed men and dream of the glamour of a soldier's life, presumably as a way of asserting their manhood or as a romanticised search for freedom and power. Graça Machel, an expert appointed by the UN Secretary-General to explore the situation of children affected by war, explained that "young people often take up arms to gain power and power can act as a very strong motivator in situations where people feel powerless and are otherwise unable to acquire basic resources."[17]

No one would say that it is good for children to join the armed forces, but a report on the reintegration of war-affected youth in Sierra Leone suggests that sometimes choosing to go with the soldiers or rebels makes sense to the child: "The process [of recruiting underage combatants] began in Kailahun as early as April 1991. . . . Many of these youngsters had lost parents or guardians in the first wave of RUF [Revolutionary United Front] attacks. Some were motivated to fight by desire for revenge, and found in military training a substitute for lost family support and educational opportunity. The [children] call their recruiting officer (in Krio) *bra* ("elder brother"). The bond that emerges between bra and apprentice fighter (*borbor* = "small boy") is sometimes as strong as that between child and parent or guardian."[18]

The standard picture of a child soldier is that of a child who fights and kills. However, when former child soldiers are interviewed, only some claim to have killed people (usually a small number, such as up to three killings), and very few report killing many people (such as up to twenty killings). What about the others? With the scarcity of equipment characterizing African armies and paramilitaries, many children staying with armed groups are not even given a weapon, so one must assume that the majority of their time must be spent doing other things than fighting and killing. What has typically been described as "child soldiering" is in reality more correctly defined as "children associated with armed groups," and this definition is also becoming increasingly adopted by the child rights community. Like in other male-dominated environments in Africa, children in armed forces mainly conduct so-called support services. These normally include cooking, washing laundry, fetching water, and doing dishes—the same activities a child carries out in normal circumstances—as well as transporting equipment, food, and ammunition, which can be devastatingly heavy and energy-demanding.[19] A role often given to children, because of their natural advantage over adults, is that of messenger or spy. As a rebel commander put it, "They're very good at getting information. You can send them across enemy lines and nobody suspects them [because] they're so young." While this role may seem less life-threatening than others, it has a serious consequence, as it puts all children under suspicion. Children are also used for watching over their units' food and equipment, a task that does not require them to be armed, but that does imply serious risks. A 10-year-old boy from Burundi said: "We spent sleepless nights watching for the enemy. My first role was to carry a torch for grown-up rebels. Later I was shown how to use hand grenades."[20]

An additional serious issue related to children's participation in armed forces has recently become documented, namely sexual abuse.

Younger recruits are often forced to provide the older combatants with sexual services. This pattern is facilitated by a military command structure under which obeying orders and respecting those with higher rank are fundamental characteristics. The gross power inequality between a child and an adult combatant leaves young recruits with little choice. In the perverse environment of war, children also have strong incentives for complying, and even play a seductive role. Children in extreme situations around the world have proven an ability to develop sexual coping strategies used to calm their tormentors, often in order to stay alive or to prevent even worse pain. "Voluntary" sexual submission to a ranking officer can also serve as a survival strategy and be a way for child recruits to gain protection against other combatants and privileges like food, less hazardous assignments, and eventually, access to arms.

The majority of children found within armed forces are boys, but there is also a surprisingly high number of girls.[21] The girls found within armed forces are more often victims of abduction compared to boys. They rarely carry weapons and are primarily employed in supporting services (cooking, washing, etc.). However, there is little doubt that the main reason why armed groups kidnap and keep girls is to use them as sexual objects for the combatants. Concy Abanya, a 14-year-old girl abducted in Kitgum, northern Uganda, by the Lord's Resistance Army (LRA) and taken to Sudan, said: "In Sudan we were distributed to men and I was given to a man who had just killed his woman. . . . I was not given a gun, but I helped in the abductions and grabbing food from villagers. Girls who refused to become LRA wives were killed in front of us as a warning to the rest of us."[22]

Street Children

My five brothers and sisters have never been to school. I dropped out of primary because my parents couldn't afford the school fees. I'm not doing anything at the moment, but I want to become a seamstress. I'd like to do my apprenticeship in Takoradi, because it's not too far away. I'm hoping that my parents will give me money to go. I don't know how much I need, but 20,000 cedis [about $9 at that time, mid-1999] should be enough. It doesn't matter if I have to sleep on the street. Anything is better than staying here. There's no future here.[23]

The above quote is taken from Eric Beauchemin's report "The Exodus," which describes the migration of rural children to urban areas in Ghana. In a simple way, the quote describes the frustration of many rural children throughout Africa who see no fate worse than staying in their villages and would do almost anything to get out of them. The growing inequality between the rural and urban standard of living, and the stories told by those who have been to the cities, fuel children's disillusionment and their desire to leave.[24] It is not surprising, therefore, that some of these unhappy children find their way to the cities. Once there, life generally turns out to be a lot harder than expected, and many end up in the street.

There are relatively fewer street children in Africa than in Asia or Latin America, for three main reasons: fewer people live in cities; the predominantly unindustrialized production systems create a high demand for child labor; and therefore the extended family structures have a high absorption capacity for excess children. Yet African street children still constitute a considerable group, and their life situation is often extremely dramatic. Their numbers are also sharply increasing, mainly as a result of widespread violent conflict and the AIDS pandemic, both of which produce dispossessed children with no place to go but the streets.

Are the street children also working children? Of course. If they did not work they could not eat. Struggling for daily survival, street children are often ready to do anything for money, or even for some scraps of food. They may work as porters, run errands, help at construction sites or other workplaces, and wash or watch cars and mopeds. Sometimes they even have their own small businesses, such as shining shoes or selling chewing gum and Kleenex at intersections with traffic lights. They also beg, steal, or prostitute themselves if they need to and when the chance presents itself. In some cases, children have contact with adults, parents, or guardians who protect, supervise, and control their labor. In other cases, children are on their own.

It is common to divide street children into two categories: the "children *in* the street," who spend considerable time in the street but have a place to go at night, and the "children *of* the street," who have nowhere else to go and for whom the street is their home. In reality, again, many children find themselves somewhere between the two categories. In 1997 the United Nations Center for Human Settlement in Nairobi estimated that "street children represent 10–20% of the urban child population in Africa, and streets are workplace, playground and even home to as many as 16 million African children and will be to over 30 million by the year 2000." This estimate would probably fit the definition for children *in* the street, while the estimate for children *of* the street would be much lower. If we were to say, conservatively, that 10 percent of the sum above referred to children *of* the street, this would amount to about

These three street boys in Ouagadougou are only 5, 6, and 8 years old. With hopeful eyes they watch a woman cooking her evening meal.

3 million children. Ethiopia, Kenya, and South Africa would probably account for two-thirds of them, while Nigeria, Côte d'Ivoire, and the Democratic Republic of Congo would add a considerable population.

It would be too simple, however, to suggest that there are only two *types* of children on the African streets: African street children are indeed far from a homogeneous group. To begin, their backgrounds, and therefore the reasons why they are in the street, are very diverse. A tentative list of categories of street child could comprise the following:

> Children from very poor households or households in crisis working as street vendors or market aids.
> "Placed" children and domestic servants also working as street vendors.
> Neglected children from dysfunctional households.
> Homeless children living in the street with their family or siblings.

Talibé children begging and working to earn money for their own
survival and for their quranic teachers.
"Mafia children," whose labor is monitored by organized gangs.
Unaccompanied rural migrant children.
Children living in shelters who are out in the streets during the day.
Runaways.
Drug addicts.
AIDS and war orphans.
Refugee children.
Former child soldiers.

Having studied African street children for years, sociologist Yves
Marguerat concludes that the phenomenon tends to follow a fairly predictable evolutionary pattern that can be described in five steps:[25]

- *Step 1: Initial uncertainty.* There are only a few children living in
the street, people are generally unaware of what they do, and the children don't relate much to each other. This is the typical situation in
many smaller cities and capitals in Africa today (e.g., Nouakchott).
- *Step 2: Stabilization.* People are starting to notice the situation
and view the children as a nuisance. The children must defend themselves and their property against each other. There are no organized relations between the children, but there is systematic (sexual) abuse of the
younger by the older (e.g., Cotonou, Lomé).
- *Step 3: Structuring.* Organization in permanent, often extremely
violent gangs around powerful leaders. The gang contract: protection
against submission. Strong internal solidarity and development of common gang codes—hairstyle, tattoos, clothing. Drug consumption is common (e.g., Bujumbura, Abidjan, Dakar).
- *Step 4: Feminization.* The first girls join the gangs, often as the
girlfriends of the leaders. This stage is still rare in Africa, as girls tend to
be able to afford a room using their prostitution money (e.g., Kinshasa).
- *Step 5: Countersociety.* Emergence of a youth countersociety that
exists in parallel to normal society and in total breach of the national
culture. Bonds with the biological family or ethnicity cease to exist.
Children are born in the street, normally having a short life expectancy,
and in turn bear their own children in the street.

The final step is typical of the large cities in Latin America (Rio de
Janeiro, Mexico City) and seldom, if ever, found in Africa. But judging
from the words of a social worker in Ghana, Africa may be approaching
a street child countersociety faster than one may think: "I'm seeing the

third generation of street children. The grandmother came to the streets when she was young. Her children were born on the streets of Accra. One of her daughters met a boy who was also born on the streets, and they recently had a child . . . on the streets."[26]

PART 2

CONSEQUENCES AND CURES

6

Consequences

―――――――――― ▬▬ ――――――――――

On Culture and Science

While sitting under the mango tree it has become almost unbearably hot even in the shade. That is, at least to us. Some of the local children do not really seem to be bothered, running around in the sun apparently unaffected by its burning rays. Our discussion partners, however, have started to send us worried glances—can the foreigners take this heat? We brace ourselves and smile: Of course we can. If they can, we can. They send someone to fetch some more Coca-Cola. Who? A child, of course.

Child-rearing practices around the world are a result of cultural practices inherited from generation to generation. As child psychiatrist Alice Miller puts it: "Good child rearing is not something that comes natural to parents: what comes natural to parents is to raise their children the way they were raised themselves."[1] The common argument that "it is our culture to raise our children the way we do" implies that people of other cultures need to be careful about criticizing the local ways of doing things. And as an outsider, one indeed needs to be cautious, since habits incomprehensible to the foreign eye may have not only cultural functions, but also very rational and practical ones.

With the exception of extreme cases like child slavery and ritual infanticide, the most legitimate reason to encourage someone to challenge local ways of child rearing is hard scientific knowledge about the requirements of healthy child development. New scientific insight has been and should continue to be a catalyst for changing practices and behaviors around the world. Consider some changes in Western societies: Not long ago, European and American physicians would recommend that children stay out all day in the sun, because it was believed to be a good way to provide them with vitamin D. Then it was discovered that excessive exposure to ultraviolet rays can eventually cause skin cancer. Based on this new knowledge, behavior changed drastically and we now expect European and American parents to protect their children's fair skin.

At least certain types of scientific knowledge are a communication ground that can help cut through cultural barriers because of their demonstrably a-cultural nature. We were amazed by the constructive discussion generated among Africans by comparing x-ray photos of the brains of malnourished children to those of the well nourished: the damage is striking. Similarly, we discussed the fate of Muhamed Ali, the fragility of the head, and pictures of the brain showing trauma received from blows. A group of African primary school teachers could easily see the dark spots showing dead brain tissue, and came to their own conclusions about the wisdom of beating children on the head to teach them a lesson. Communicated in the right way, scientific knowledge can often be easily understood and absorbed in a local cultural setting—without necessarily challenging the culture itself. For example, instead of instructing people to follow a certain diet, it is possible to explain the negative developmental effects of poor nutrition and leave the floor open for local improvements.

Improvements in child-rearing practices throughout the world are in part due to the realization of their negative impact, and this realization comes primarily from scientific knowledge, and in general from education. In Africa the education level is considerably lower than in the rest of the world, and access to scientific knowledge is even more restricted. Thus, although international efforts to establish universal normative standards for child rights deserve all our support, they may be far more effective when combined with some knowledge transfer aimed to induce behavioral change—a change that does not copy Western behavior, but that takes place based on acknowledgment and happens within the cultural framework of a given society.

African child-rearing practices may seem tough to a Western eye and, as we have stressed, the hardship may in many cases be seen as a goal in itself. The key question: Is such hardship really always necessary? Overprotection of children or "Western-style" child-rearing may very well make many rural African children less fit for survival. Learning to work hard from an early age and to suppress the pain of heavy tasks and disease may help children develop survival skills badly needed in times of typical African hardship, during which a native would easily outsurvive a "spoiled" Westerner. However, child and adolescent mortality rates in Africa are high, and would no doubt be lower if children worked less, in less dangerous places, and didn't have to work when ill. Much attention has been given to the mortality of infants and children under age 5. But the age distribution of six African countries shown in Figure 6.1 suggests that the mortality rate of children tends to remain quite high up to 15 years of age, and then drop and stabilize in late adolescence. In other words, mortality rates are still high among "working-age" children.

The challenge becomes finding the right balance between developing locally necessary survival skills on the one hand, and maximizing good child development on the other. To put it brutally: to determine the acceptable balance for how many will have to sink for the others to learn to swim. While hardships can be valuable, it may be fruitful to try to separate between "good hardships," understood as challenges that develop discipline, experience, and motivation, and "bad hardships," understood to harm the physically and psychologically healthy develop-

Figure 6.1 Partial age pyramids showing percentage of population 0–29 years old in six African countries

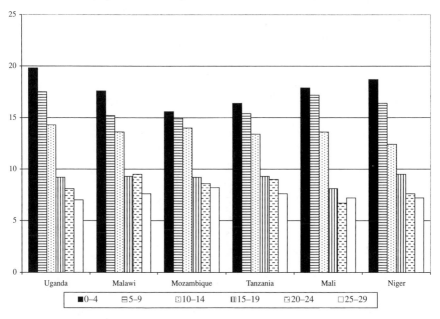

Source: Own calculations based on Macro International data.

ment of children. In the first category are several tasks entrusted to children to help out their family that are not harmful in terms of the definition of child labor presented in Chapter 1. Schoolwork is also a type of labor that can be challenging and help children develop good focus, motivation, and discipline. "Bad hardships" are labor tasks that fall under any of the thirty-five points of harmfulness presented in Chapter 1, because they hamper the physical, psychological, moral, and cognitive development of the child, and interfere with the development of the child's identity and self.

Physiological Effects

A child's skeleton is soft and not yet fully shaped. The nervous system—including the brain—is still developing. Physicians, biologists, and physiotherapists have for decades carefully examined these developmental processes, leading to an extensive knowledge about what can harm and what can promote a child's healthy physiological development. Some working children face greater risks of having their physiological development hampered than do other children, because they are more likely to be exposed to a number of harmful factors such as physical stress, dangerous substances, and accidents. To be sure, not all work is bad for physiological development. If performed with moderation and informed supervision, work may strengthen the bodies of children the same way as playing sports. And inactivity may in many cases be just as harmful as exhaustion, leading for instance to heart problems and obesity—something that has become an important concern in many developed countries. Overall, we believe that working hinders the healthy physical growth of large numbers of African children in the following main ways:

1. *Working too hard.* A most basic requirement for good child development is energy to grow, and this energy needs to come from a healthy and balanced diet. A hardworking child will need more energy than a less active child, since the body will burn a higher amount of calories during the work process. With insufficient energy left for growth, the child's physiological development will suffer. Working can therefore be particularly harmful for a malnourished child. But hard work does not present a risk only when food is inadequate. For instance, children who work in agriculture and construction tend to be assigned tasks of lifting objects that are too heavy for their skeletal system, and the ILO also points out that young apprentices are often taught harmful working posi-

Work that is too heavy or too hard may be not only painful, but also overly demanding of the energy and resources that a child needs for healthy physiological development.

tions that, when sustained for many hours, may lead to skeletal malformations with implications for the muscular system. In the long run, physiological harm may lead to chronic pain, repetitive strain injury, and even disability.

2. *Illness and insufficient time to recover.* Due to a rough climate, low water quality, insufficient immunization, and underdeveloped sanitation systems, African children have the highest incidence of disease in the world. Diarrhea, malaria, acute respiratory infections, and lately also HIV/AIDS-related illnesses are particularly common. The body needs energy to combat these diseases, and it also needs a certain time to recover. Failing to rest during a disease or to give the body time to recover is likely to lead to prolonged illness, complications, additional infections, relapses, and sometimes even chronic conditions or permanent harm. Ignorance about these risks is particularly worrisome in a

cultural context where the "hardship-makes-you-strong" ideology rules.
    3. *Environmental hazards*. During a visit to a gold mine, we were
told the story of a young boy named Aaron and his older brother. One
day Aaron had not come up from a deep vein, so his older brother was
sent to look for him. When neither Aaron nor his brother came back, one
more miner was sent to look for them. It was only after this man did not
come back either that it became apparent that subterranean gasses had
killed all three. This story may illustrate the worst-case scenario, but
many children are exposed to unhealthy substances in the places where
they work. Particularly exposed are children who work in mines, children who labor in workshops, children who apply insecticides or work
on farms that use agrochemicals, children who sell gas, and children
who work in places with heavy exhaust from engines (street children,
for example). Children in Tanzanian mines are also reportedly exposed
to radiation, and they are probably not the only ones.[2] In 2002 the
International Institute of Tropical Agriculture (IITA) surveyed cocoa
farms in four West African countries and concluded that 142,000 children were involved in pesticide application in Côte d'Ivoire alone.
There is no reason to believe that cocoa or Côte d'Ivoire are any worse
than many other crops and countries in this respect.[3] Chemical exposure
can cause severe developmental effects and even be lethal, whether
instantly or in a relatively short term. Not only may internal organs and
physical growth be hampered, but exposure to many substances that are
frequently used without responsible supervision may cause damages to
the nervous system that, in the long run, can lead to mental, psychological, as well as cognitive malfunctioning. Reduced fertility or infertility
may also occur, as for instance in the case of children who inhale gasoline.
    4. *Accidents*. Fouseini, a talibé boy, was injured while working in
his master's fields. His wound was never treated, and when we met him,
six months later, his leg had started to rot and the bone was showing. He
was weakened by infection and malnutrition, and malaria had become
an almost permanent condition, since his immune system seemed to
have closed down. In workshops and farms, children frequently hurt
themselves with tools they are too young and uncoordinated to handle,
like machetes, welding equipment, and electrical machinery. Sores and
wounds often go untreated, and may cause infections that may have
lethal consequences. In 2002 the IITA estimated that 146,000 children
under the age of 15 were using machetes to clear cocoa farms in Côte
d'Ivoire, Nigeria, Ghana, and Cameroon alone.[4] Serious risks of accidents have been documented, particularly at construction sites and in
mines, where children without protective equipment have suffered falls.

But even workplaces that we tend to think are less dangerous can have a high risk for accidents. Working in and around households, for instance, can be risky for children, with burns and cuts being a frequent consequence of tending to open fires, boiling water, and hot oil, and using knives and other sharp kitchenware from a young age.

To make things worse, working children typically face a combination of several of these health risks, which together obviously pose a risk of negative synergies, as in the case of Fouseini, the talibé boy. It is a major problem that many supervising adults, and even more so the children themselves, have little idea of the risks and consequences of their work situations.

Psychological Effects

Good mental health implies not only the absence of mental illness and psychiatric disorders, but also balanced self-esteem and sound self-confidence—that is, a realistic perception of one's own capacity as well as the ability to analyze constructively and respond adequately to one's surroundings. Mental hospitals around the world are full of individuals

This young boy is selling gas. While sucking gasoline into the hose to create a vacuum, he inhales fumes that can be highly toxic.

who, following childhood abuse, have developed serious psychiatric disturbances and neuroses, and have more or less lost their grasp on reality. Self-esteem can be inadequately or perversely developed in children who don't feel loved and valued, with the effect that they either systematically continue to expose themselves to exploitation and abuse as adults, or later on repeat the abuse pattern by transferring their own pain to those over whom they have power—the main candidates being their offspring and spouse. Children who grow up with deception and manipulation learn to distrust their own intuition, something that creates a fragile self-confidence, often expressed by great insecurity vis-à-vis their own ability to interpret their surroundings. Negative childhood experiences can even produce physiological manifestations, and may be expressed by adrenaline rush, heart palpitations, or trembling triggered by the slightest cues. While such reactions could be useful within certain extremely threatening surroundings, they are not in most settings, and may instead lead to extreme stress and irrational fear and aggression.

Child labor, and perhaps more often the life situation in which much of Africa's child labor takes place, is an experience that inevitably affects children psychologically, for better or for worse.[5] As with other childhood experiences, its impact will be mediated by the child's personality—that is, his or her biological preconditions. The more naturally resilient a child is, the better he or she will be able to handle negative experiences. However, the marvelous nature of children makes them tremendously adaptive, and this ability is exactly what makes them vulnerable to the long-term damaging effects of negative exposure. This is why we fear that the prevailing "sink-or-swim" approach to African child rearing may result in an alarmingly high number of children who sink psychologically compared to those who learn to swim. However, let us begin by looking at the potentially positive psychological impact of child labor.

"When I was her age, I would have never dreamed of responding this way to my mother" is a known refrain for many of today's parents in all societies. Grandparents throughout the Western Hemisphere often express their disappointment in the lax pedagogical standards used with their grandchildren. Similarly, many non-Westerners would say that European and American child-rearing practices have become far too lenient, and some suggest that adult Westerners seem to have turned into the servants of their own children. Overconcern for the fragility of the child and overeagerness to follow the latest theories on child development can easily result in excessive protection or permissiveness. In addition, Western children often grow up in a world fairly isolated from the professional lives of their parents, and even children who are not yet in school tend to be only marginally involved in the work of the households where they spend their time.

Sociologists say that satisfaction comes from a good balance between *abilities* and *demand.* It is easy to imagine the frustration arising from a situation where the demand constantly exceeds a child's abilities. However, it is easy to forget that frustration may also come out of a situation where the child's abilities are never seriously challenged. In Chapter 4, when discussing child labor in the commercial labor market, for example, we quoted Aman, the Somali girl, who frequently expresses great enthusiasm and satisfaction over the opportunity to help out her mother and her two siblings with her earnings. It is obvious that some of Aman's different work experiences help her develop confidence and courage, and an ability to maneuver more successfully in her environment.

A certain detachment from the adult world of labor and responsibility leaves plenty of room for play (and later for study), possibly leading to good cognitive and creative development. But excessive separation may also leave the child with the impression that he or she doesn't matter or contribute to the family. The result is a feeling of dependency and uselessness. Even though this feeling may not always be explicitly recognized and reflected upon, it is certain that children who don't work only rarely enjoy the satisfaction that their working peers experience when they can conclude that they have mastered a productive skill, or that they are valued contributors to their family's welfare. While many African kids may feel they are an integral part of a group, most Western children have learned to expect to be passively served and provided for until adulthood.

We develop our identity and self in interaction with others, and based on the responses of our surroundings. Cross-cultural research shows that work plays an important role in shaping children's personality, and in teaching them behaviors considered appropriate for their gender. In many African societies it may also provide for the development of relationships that will determine lifelong commitments.[6] However, many child work situations do not provide the type of feedback that could help children develop sound self-esteem and a generally positive attitude toward life and labor. This becomes even more serious considering that many children live in their workplaces (like many child domestics, talibés, and miners) or spend considerable time there (like many apprentices, street vendors, and restaurant workers). Although constant physical exhaustion and pain may be strongly demoralizing, it is the work situation more often than the labor itself that poses the strongest threat to children's healthy psychosocial development.

Let's consider some features of work situations that can work to the detriment of the self-esteem, self-confidence, and even mental health of a child. The tough hierarchies found among, for instance, groups of apprentices or street children are often reinforced by the humiliation of those at the bottom of the ladder, perhaps strengthening the resilience of some, but also squashing the self-confidence of those who are less resilient. Many of the children we've met also feel that they are being treated unfairly, but have no alternative but to swallow their anger. Typically, they have not been paid the salary they were promised, often after accusations of theft or simply poor performance. Among miner boys, information about employers not to be trusted is in high demand, as many boys have had bad experiences. Even worse are the situations where the child is regularly tricked or manipulated by the employer, who may even challenge the child's very perception of reality, forcing the child to admit to having committed offenses he or she has not. In addition, it is not unusual for working children to be on their own and therefore feel unprotected and scared. Thus it is not surprising that children involved in the worst forms of child labor (at mining sites, in the streets, in armed conflicts, in brothels) are frequent users of drugs, quite clearly responding to their feelings of fear, insecurity, and frustration. Obviously, rather than representing a solution to a psychologically stressful situation, drugs cause additional stress, and may ultimately become the main cause of later mental and emotional disorder.

Most children will at some level experience a sense of deception and abandonment when their parents or closest relatives decide to send them away from home. While they may cry for a short period and then adjust to the new situation, the traces of this feeling of being unwanted linger on in the psyche, and can easily be reinforced if the child in his or her new workplace meets a lack of care and consideration. Even children who are not sent to live away from home may experience a similar deception. One of our consultants, Julius, now in his 40s, told us that he will never forget the day in his childhood when he came home crying after having been badly beaten by his employer, only to be taken back by force by his own father. Julius's eyes even today express a flash of grief and disbelief when recalling the story. His unusual mental strength and resilience, however, prevented the sad reaction that will come about in so many children: the conviction that a beating is justified and the consecutive downgrading of one's value and self, which can irreparably damage children's psychosocial health. Children tend to know intuitively when something is wrong. By manipulating and overruling a child's intuition over a long period of time, one of the most important sensory mechanisms of humans can become harmed or even destroyed. It is thus perhaps not the exaggerated physical punishment and harassment of working children that are most threatening for mental health—real harm happens the day the children themselves become convinced that this is what they deserve, the day the voice of intuition telling them that "This is not fair!" is silenced for good.

Maltreatment and Harmful Discipline

"When would you consider it to be right for me to beat my child?" The young village pastor has so far been silently sitting on the edge of our group under the mango tree with his wife and firstborn child. Knowing how touchy most people tend to be on issues regarding their children, our safest answer is another question: "When would you feel that you had to?" He ponders briefly and says: "Well, for instance, when the child gets too close to the open well. We have to make sure that he stays away from the well. I cannot bear the thought of him falling into it." "Then why don't you cover up the well?" we ask, but his befuddled expression makes it clear that the thought had never crossed his mind. In many Western societies we protect our children primarily by making sure that their environment is safe—child-proof bottle caps, cabinet locks, gates for the stairs. Protecting children from all sorts of danger in risky African environments would probably constitute an excessive challenge. Instead, the accent becomes to somehow teach children to protect themselves, first of all by making safe decisions. *What comes natural is to raise your child the way you were raised yourself.*

Physical punishment is a rather labor-saving way to convey a lesson, and is common all over Africa. Traditional wisdom recommends it as a fundamental ingredient of good upbringing and most adults use it, whether they are the child's parents, teachers, or employers. Indeed, many Africans see the Western trend of discouraging—or even forbidding—physical punishment as a sign of decadence and the reason behind many modern evils. Even in the scientific community there is considerable disagreement on the effects of corporal punishment. While most child researchers will agree that hitting a child's head can cause serious harm and should be avoided, only a minority would defend spanking, a larger group an occasional slap, while the most moderate would oppose any physical punishment, perceiving it as "a violation of the dignity of the child." Many also feel that the relationship between corporal punishment and the children's later tendency toward mental imbalance, violence, and crime has been documented well enough to deter the practice all together.

As an alternative to explaining to the child why certain behaviors should be avoided, a slap or a hit over the head is obviously a quick and easy way to make a point. If someone is unaware of the physiological consequences and, moreover, is convinced that experiencing hardship is the most effective way to learn, it would certainly be difficult to change this habit. But even if a child may learn to avoid falling into a well, this learning is clearly inferior to learning by explanation. Good explanation based on communication with a child will in many cases bring much more sustainable behavioral change. Young apprentices with whom we have talked had often—though not always— understood what they had done wrong when they were punished, but they were not told what they should have done instead. Selim, a 12-year-old working in a garage, was hit for having passed to his master the wrong tool, but was never told what the right tool would have been and why.

The latter point is also important within the medical debate on the negative psychological consequences of corporal punishment. If children understand why they are being punished, they will also soon become capable of mapping the type of behavior that is likely to provoke the pain. In other words, there is an element of predictability that increases the child's feeling of control over his or her situation, and this appears to be valuable even if the child is not capable of avoiding the wrongdoing. The worst long-term consequences seem to stem from unsystematic and mood-based responses: a relatively "serious" offense will go unnoticed one day and be heavily punished another, while a seemingly innocent act can occasionally provoke a major reaction. The constant fear and insecurity produced by such randomness have proven far more detrimental to children than perhaps excessive but nevertheless predictable punishment.[7]

With the pervasiveness of corporal punishment in Africa, are working children more at risk of (excessive) punishment and maltreatment? While we have not been able to find rigorous evidence one way or another, our experience suggests that they may well be. This is because, more often than not, the hardest-working children are also the ones enjoying the lowest status in the pecking order: stepchildren, orphans, servants, apprentices, and the like. Those separated from their families are particularly at risk of becoming the target of a master's frustrations. Take the case of child domestic servants. Their low status and the fact that they are always present in the employer's home and have few other places to go, simply make them the natural victim of the outbursts of any household member, regardless of whether they themselves have in any way contributed to the bad mood.

So while occasional slapping is probably very common, there is also reason to believe that many child workers are exposed to much more serious abuse. For example, we have seen a surprising number of former servant girls who seem to have had their hands or wrists broken, leading us to suppose that the punishment of Odile (pictured below), whose hands were crushed by her employer, is far from rare. In the same shelter as Odile was a 5-year-old girl named Yvette, whose hand was amputated after being deliberately burned, to teach the girl not to steal. We have also seen broken ribs and collarbones that were never properly set, often causing permanent infections and pain. At times, the maltreatment of working children leads to death, but the young victims are often so far from caring kin that the cases go unreported. Even when the cases are reported, legal action is seldom pursued, and perpetrators rarely punished. A notable exception is the case of a minister's wife in Benin who beat her child servant to death and ended up in jail.[8]

Odile is a 10-year-old child domestic servant. As punishment for buying the wrong brand of beer, her mistress crushed her hands and beat her jaws. Hitting the head and hands is among the most common ways that African child workers are punished.

Sexual Abuse

> Sexually abused children often make drawings of themselves without hands—that is, as helpless.[9]

It is extremely difficult to research sexual abuse, and consequently, most evidence stems from qualitative studies and is based on few case studies.[10] There is very little statistical information on the sexual abuse of children in Africa. A researcher cannot simply start surveying a large number of children on whether they have been exposed to sexual assaults, and in any case, the likelihood that the child will tell a stranger is very slim. Spending time to gain the child's confidence will make large-scale research very costly. Besides, should a child actually decide to talk about sexual abuse, the researcher cannot simply end the interview by dismissing the child with a "Thanks, that was really helpful." A child who has spoken up has reopened a wound and will need help. In other words, to start digging into children's traumas requires a solid support system, again multiplying the costs of the research.

Sexual abuse of children, in general, tends to be relatively common when societies are under stress from conflict, unemployment, poverty, social disintegration, or just a general feeling of powerlessness. It should therefore not be too risky to assume that sexual abuse of children is quite common throughout Africa. The spread patterns of HIV/AIDS seem to confirm this hypothesis, as children born HIV-negative later become infected. Although common, the sexual abuse of children is not tolerated by African culture. The Baifa and the Beti in Cameroon, for instance, refer to a child who has been raped as "one who has been decayed"—physically interpreted as a destruction of the child's immature genitals and psychologically interpreted as the destruction of the child's identity: a spiritual death.[11] It is hard to claim for sure that working children are at higher risk of sexual abuse than are nonworking children. For example, there is growing evidence of widespread sexual abuse of children in African schools. Among South Africa's young rape victims, almost 38 percent pointed to their schoolteacher or principal as the perpetrator,[12] and the World Organization Against Torture reports that teachers frequently submit Congolese girls to sexual violence.[13] The progression of HIV/AIDS incidence confirms the high frequency of sexual interactions between teachers and students—at all levels of schooling. So does the risk really increase if the child works?

The answer is probably yes, if the child is separated from his or her family or is from very humble origins, because in such cases children will be at their most vulnerable and social mechanisms that deter potential aggressors will be at their weakest. Probably the most powerful deterrent is societal reaction. The violation of a child is often seen as an offense to the entire family, or a whole lineage, something that is very well in line with the general collective thinking of African culture. The traditional reaction would be for the family of the victim to take the case to the family of the perpetrator, and for the two families to negotiate a deal with regard to compensation.[14] If the negotiations are difficult, a community council can be involved and a traditional trial held.

Not all cases are ever settled or even brought up, and an important reason for this is the very fragility of many Africa societies. Rocking the boat, in the sense of bringing forth a conflict with another family, potentially poses serious risks and social costs in closely intertwined and interdependent communities. The family of the victim is thus forced to value its love and support for the violated child against the risks of raising a case against another family. It is easy to see, therefore, how confronting an employer—perhaps one who employs several family members—may be risky. As a result, many cases go unreported and unsettled, either because the child is not considered worth the bother, or because the bother is simply unthinkable, regardless of the affection the parents may have for the child.[15] On the beautiful but infamous slave port island of Goré, facing Dakar, children often work as tourist guides, meeting incoming boats and accompanying the visitors for a walk around to the historic sites. In the French newspaper *Libération* on October 22, 1997, Jean Gortais wrote: "In Goré black children are victims of white pedophiles . . . the population suffers; the inhabitants know and talk among themselves, but they fear the potential reactions of the white and of public officials. They don't dare to complain and even less to press charges."

Among children at high risk of sexual abuse are street venders and domestic servants. According to some of our research, abuse by the father in an employing household is probably less common than often thought, possibly because the child domestic comes under the direct authority of the mother, who makes sure to minimize contact between her husband and the child domestic.[16] On the other hand, research indicates that older boys in the household or related to members of the household more often become the perpetrators. Without proper supervision and care in the employing household, girls, often starved for attention and affection, are an easy target, whether by seduction or force. In any case, the chance that anyone will make trouble by standing up for the child is slim. Quite the contrary, we have seen child domestics scolded or fired after neighbor women have complained that the child has "seduced" their husbands. It has also been documented that market women mediate the sexual services of their consenting child domestics or shop helpers, and that way function as their pimps, keeping the money for themselves.[17]

Children in the worst types of child labor are obviously at a much higher risk for sexual assault than all other groups of children, but it is important to recall that they represent a very small and extreme group of working children. As mentioned, venereal diseases flourish among children in many mining sites, indicating a high incidence of sexual abuse in such disintegrated and male-dominated societies. A prominent function of children who work within armed forces is to provide sexual services. This puts them at high risk of contracting sexually transmitted diseases (STDs), as soldiers globally have an incidence of STDs than is two to five times higher than the rate in the civilian population.[18] For example, almost all the girls who had escaped the Lord Resistance Army in northern Uganda were found to be suffering from STDs.[19] Street children, as well, are at extreme risk, and not only in the streets where they sleep and work. They are systematically violated by adults and older boys, and often even by the very policemen and social workers who were supposed to provide protection. Moreover, street children and other children exploited in illicit activities covered under the "worst forms of child labor" of ILO Convention 182 are reported to suffer sexual abuse in prisons and detention centers, by both prison officials and other prisoners. A horrifying report from Malawi revealed that prison officials were paid to smuggle children from the juvenile block to the male prison, and that the "buyer" then made money by "renting out" the child to the other inmates. Almost all inmates with peri-anal abscesses were under 18 years old, and half the prisoners who visited the medical center were HIV-positive.[20]

Physical injuries are among the common consequences of sexual abuse, often all over the body, but particularly in the vagina, mouth, and rectum. Because in children these areas of the body are easily torn, they are more susceptible to sexually transmitted diseases, putting them at a high risk of contracting everything from HIV/AIDS and syphilis to scabies and pubic lice. Many sexually abused girls also end up with unwanted pregnancies, particularly in cases of extended abuse. Needless to say, pregnancy among young, poor, and often socially excluded girls involves considerable health risks, in addition to the trauma connected to giving birth to the baby of a rapist. Psychological reactions to sexual abuse tend to vary with the type of abuse, the age of the child, the child's resilience, and the support the child receives. Very young children tend to withdraw into themselves, since they have a limited capaci-

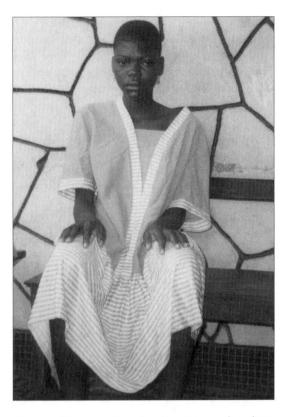

The pressure and exposure in many labor situations become too much to bear for some children. What happened to this former child domestic servant? We don't know. She doesn't talk anymore.

ty to assess and interpret the traumatic experience. Abused children frequently suffer from depression, nightmares and sleep disorders, anxiety and fears, guilt, and self-blame. They therefore often develop learning problems as well as problems with social adjustment, including an inability to develop healthy and respectful relationships with the opposite sex. Because of fear and shame, sexually abused children rarely seek help. On the contrary, they may react by developing what the surrounding community interprets as promiscuous behavior, often in a desperate and misguided effort to attract affection, but also as a way to simulate strength and toughness in a situation of extreme vulnerability. This behavior will later encourage repeated abuse and then, in turn, serve to bring blame to the child for encouraging the abuse.

When not protected by their family, very few children are aware of their legal rights, and rarely think about taking their abuse cases to court. As a probation officer in a juvenile court in Kenya said to Human Rights Watch: "Kids don't think of appealing, they think of escaping. Even if they are told that they have 14 days to appeal, they don't, they only think of escaping. They don't even understand what appealing means."[21]

Educational Effects

While most African children tend to combine school and work, labor demands sometime keep children out of school altogether. This is either because there really is a lot of work to do at home or because the adults of the household simply like to have the help of a child at hand when—or if—something needs doing. Children may also be put to work in times of crisis, but these cases are probably less common in Africa than in Asia and Latin America, because most African child labor is unpaid and family controlled. When asked why their children were never sent to school, three-fourths of Ethiopian parents gave as their first or second reason that their children were needed to work on the family farm or around the household. In comparison, only 8 percent gave as their main reason that school was too expensive, and only 5 percent referred to the long distance to school.[22]

Household demand for the labor—or for just the presence—of school-aged children can also lead to late enrollment, low grades, repetition, and early dropout. A survey of children working on cocoa farms in Côte d'Ivoire shows that those who combined school with work were on average 1.6 years older than children who only went to school, presumably because of later enrollment and because they had higher repetition rates.[23] Similarly, a study on schoolchildren in Tanzania found that labor systematically reduced their reading abilities and mathematical skills.[24] In Ghana, children who worked scored worse than nonworking children on basic reading and math tests, with children who worked outside the household performing particularly poorly.[25]

Of course, the amount and type of work children do make a difference in school performance, as does their resilience. But it also matters to what extent the child's labor is accommodated to fit with schooling, and vice versa. Take the example of Malunga, a bright 9-year-old girl who loves going to school but seldom does her homework. She thinks she might soon drop out because she has to help her mother sell snacks during the midday break and help with housework after school hours, so the only time Malunga has for studying is after dark. With no electricity and poor vision, her eyes become swollen and red from reading in the flickering smoky light of the kerosene lamp, and in any case kerosene is too expensive to be used just for Malunga's homework. Thus far Malunga's quick wits have helped her get away with doing very little homework, but as classes become more demanding it is difficult to expect that she will be able to keep up. On the other hand, many of her classmates face similar challenges at harvest time, when they are needed in the fields and may have to skip school altogether for one or two months. Yet school calendars still tend to be very similar to those of colonial times, and therefore inspired by European seasons rather than local harvest times. Moving school holidays to coincide with times that are critical for the dominant local crop would certainly make it easier to maintain school attendance.

How important is formal education? Most people will agree that the basic skills taught in primary school can empower children and improve their opportunities later in life. However, it has been argued that the quality of schooling and the relevance of the curriculum are often so questionable that children's time could be invested more fruitfully else-where. In many African schools the curriculum seems focused on edu-cating children for unemployment, in the sense that the skills that are taught are mostly useful in the formal sector, which employs only a small fraction of the labor force.[26] Besides, the more education one receives, the harder it is to accept life as a subsistence farmer. Hence the exodus of educated rural children toward unemployment in urban areas, where street life, crime, and prostitution in many cases are the out-comes. In such a context it is not surprising that many parents still pre-fer apprenticeship arrangements with local craftsmen, or other working arrangements in which they hope their children will learn some useful skills or at least a trade that helps them stay out of trouble.

Yet statistics make it clear that, of two individuals with similar background, the one with a better education will end up with a higher income. A common way to measure this is by the so-called age-earning curves. An age-earning curve is calculated on the basis of a national sur-vey providing the income level of individuals with and without educa-tion at different ages, at a particular point in time. With income on one axis and age on the other, we can plot a curve showing the average income at various ages for individuals with different education levels. For example, Figure 6.2 shows earning curves for individuals with and without primary school in Ethiopia, ages 7 through 60. These curves have been "discounted" to take into consideration the fact that income in the future is worth less than income in the present. In fact, if a child earns a wage, the money will be available immediately and can be

Figure 6.2   Sample age earning curve based on Ethiopian data

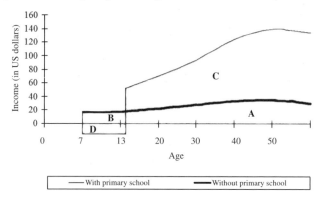

Source: World Bank 1998.

invested, while if he or she goes to primary school, the family will miss not only the child's earnings but also the cumulative interest on the earnings.[27]

Not surprisingly, throughout the primary school years, children who work generally have a higher average income than children who go to school. After that, children who completed primary school tend to have a higher income. In Figure 6.2, Field B represents the predicted income of a child who works instead of going to primary school and Field A represents the predicted income of the same child as he or she grows up. Field C, on the other hand, is the additional income of individuals who completed primary education. Even after subtracting possible expenses related to schooling (Field D), it is clear that people who finished elementary school will end up earning a lot more during their lifetime than those who did not. As economists would say, in Ethiopia there appears to be a positive return to the investment in primary education.

Although the Ethiopian case is representative of most African contexts, there are certainly exceptions to this general trend. As mentioned in Chapter 1, an age-earning curve based on a household survey from Burkina Faso actually showed a negative return to primary education, while the benefits of primary education can be extremely slim in some places, notably in rural farming communities. The explanation is often that the skills taught in the available schools were either so irrelevant for the local labor market or so inadequate for the farming sector that no welfare improvements resulted from children having been sent to school. In the first case, the children who stayed home and learned to farm ended up better-off than their educated but unemployed peers.

These cases, however, cannot overshadow the fact that education is probably the most important path to development in Africa, and even when the returns to education cannot be documented in economic terms, their social returns may be equally valuable. Moreover, the difference in future prospects between those with education and those without is likely to increase as the economy modernizes. In a modern economy, a larger formal labor market will require more formal skills, starting with literacy and numeracy. Education will thus become a much more important precondition for employment, and for achieving a well-adjusted life in general. It is not by chance that one of the first preoccupations of Africans who have emigrated to Europe or the United States is helping to improve education back in their home villages. In the remote and arid region of Kayes, in western Mali, we found some very poor villages with well-functioning elementary schools thanks to the remittances of those who had migrated to France and fully understood the importance of education for a modern economy. Because labor prevents children from going to school, and leads to repetition, poor performance, and early dropout, the children who work today are likely to become even more disadvantaged compared to their peers than yesterday's working children already are. With its high child labor rates, Africa is similarly likely to become even more disadvantaged compared to the rest of the world.[28]

7

Possible Cures

"YOU CALL IT WORK, I CALL IT HELPING OUT. WHAT'S WRONG WITH children helping out? I did it, my children do it, and their children will do it too. It has always been this way, it's our way of life." We had known Alfred, a retired teacher, for many years and he could see no reason not to be frank with us. Children's work is so much a part of African life that it is hard to imagine how things could be different in the near future. Yet Africa is changing, pushed by climatic and technological evolutions, by ongoing globalization, and also by its intellectual elites. Surely there are no obvious quick fixes either to the most common types of child labor or to its worst forms. But looking at the consequences, it is clear that a process of change needs to be initiated, for humanitarian as well as for developmental reasons. It is not just that work may interfere with children's healthy development and cause them unnecessary suffering. As African societies face rapid urbanization, increased materialism, and the disintegration of traditional community and family structures, children's work tends to slide toward its worst forms. And that, in turn, can be at best a very shortsighted development option. The exploitation of children may turn in quick benefits or profits, but in the long run it will contribute to lowering the quality of the labor force and creating a business environment not very attractive for most investors. Hence the need for an approach that considers cultural and traditional specificities, but simultaneously acknowledges that tradition and culture are evolving—sometimes very rapidly.

We think it is crucial that strategies to combat the negative aspects of child labor be seen in the larger context of optimizing child development and welfare overall. In too many countries, donors force under-staffed and underfunded governments to develop policy strategies and legal reforms related to their own, often marginal, short-term, and isolated pet issues, overwhelming weak bureaucracies with loads of paper-work that tend to make more sense in Washington, Brussels, or Geneva than in Niamey, Asmara, or Gaborone. African countries face massive child vulnerability. It is fundamental to provide all children with at least some basic services that can support their survival and development, even while there is precious little capacity to develop special policies on behalf of a dozen different subgroups of vulnerable children to secure funding from this or that source. Given the magnitude of the need and the scarcity of resources, both donors and governments must take a more global approach—it helps little to save a child from exploitation if she dies from malaria a week later. We need to be *child-focused,* not *problem-focused.* The overarching objectives for child labor policies must thus be to improve child well-being and development, not to chase children out of plantations or market stalls. Child labor is an important topic because it constitutes one of the factors that can be harmful for child welfare and development, but it is only one among several.

Where does one start? We once asked Elisée Soumonni, a professor of slavery history at the University of Benin, if we could learn some-thing relevant to child labor from the successful abolition of transat-lantic slavery. He answered that three steps had been crucial. First was the development of a humanistic antislavery movement among the users of slaves, mainly in Europe and the United States. Second came the legal abolition of the trade. Third came the enforcement of this abolition thanks to the British armada patrolling the ancient Slave Coast. The sequencing of the three was very important. A strategy to combat the negative sides of child labor could follow the same pattern. The basis must be an evolving understanding of the harmful aspects of child labor among a substantial number of principal users. Normative guidelines should then be consolidated into national and international legal frame-works to define and mandate basic child protection. Finally, the legal protection of children must be enforced, including provision of services for the children who are found in the most serious situations of exploita-tion and neglect.

Step 1: Development of an Understanding

A factor that is frequently ignored when examining history is the *sequencing* of the three steps that successfully helped combat slavery.

With regard to child labor, the impression is that the second step—a legal framework—comes first, and this framework has been receiving by far the most attention. In contrast to the process of abolishing slavery, in which the initiative was taken from within the user-communities, most legal regulations against child labor are initiated in international organizations that debate and design programs at a distance, both physically and culturally, from the intended users. Yet we know from sociologists that laws can produce social change only if the distance between the behaviors they prescribe and commonly accepted behavior is not very wide.[1] Hence the need to reduce the distance between what African societies consider acceptable behavior toward children and the normative standards sought by international experts.

What does it take to change what people find acceptable? While there are no proven recipes, the basic idea is to find a way to reach people—including children—with a message they can understand and that can engender a willingness to communicate with an open mind. At the same time, the communicators themselves must remain open to influence, even to the extent that they may revise or reconsider their original message. In development jargon, such an effort is called an "information, education, and communication" (IEC) campaign, or a "communication for behavioral change" (CBC) campaign, and in one form or another has long been part of the bag of tricks of most development organizations, especially for sectors—such as hygiene and nutrition—whose success depends heavily on the behavior of intended beneficiaries. However, IEC/CBC projects tend to appear unattractive to both donors and African governments, because results are hard to measure compared to more typical "bricks and mortar" projects, and because ribbon-cutting opportunities are greatly reduced. But communication is critical to ensure that people understand new processes to come, and that they be given the opportunity to influence them. Communication is also needed so that donors and governments may better understand the sources of the problems they are trying to solve and the concerns of the populations they are claiming to assist.

To a surprising degree we find that IEC/CBC efforts—not lecturing—are highly appreciated in poor and strained societies. It is often said that such processes provide "spaces" wherein collective self-examination can take place and wherein possible solutions to local problems and challenges can be jointly discovered. However, only in a few societies, and rather infrequently, would such local processes be initiated from within, which is understandable given the stress and demands that poverty imposes on people.

Children need to go to school. The school systems need to be made more flexible in order to allow more children to become involved in basic education. The girls pictured here are taking part in an informal evening school.

Child development issues constitute a natural context for child labor, and a shared desire for healthy child development may be the easiest entry point for breaking the ice. What are your aspirations for your children, and what are the obstacles that stand in the way of reaching them? What is the nature of these obstacles, and what can be done about them? Where children work in harmful conditions (as described by the thirty-five-point list presented in Chapter 1), the consequences can be explained and discussed—there is often no knowledge of the negative consequences of certain tasks, and there are often alternative labor forms or labor distributions that could replace the abusive ones. But before even trying, communicators need to do their best to understand why an undesired practice is there in the first place. Adult altruism and family cohesion are other good entry points for IEC/CBC processes. What were the traditional parental responsibilities? What changed? How do you feel about these changes? Should traditional values be rekindled, or do they need to be replaced by something new?

Efforts to improve the lot of working children tend to target community leaders, decisionmakers, and adults in general. But it is also increasingly recognized that children themselves have the right to be listened to when it comes to matters that concern their own well-being. After all, nobody knows the situation and needs of child laborers better than they do. Realizing that children can be important agents of change, many researchers and program designers have started to open themselves to the influence of working children's perspectives. As a result, working children are becoming more and more involved in decision-making, advisory functions, and practical project work. In Senegal, for example, the NGO Environment Development Action for the Third World has supported the development of a strong movement of child domestic servants, and this movement is currently setting up branches in other cities around the world.

But realizing that child labor can be bad is like realizing that a child is sick—it's a necessary first step, but it will certainly not make the child well. For a sick child to get better, three things need to be in place. The first is a human factor: the parents need to care enough to want to do something. The second is a knowledge factor: they need to know that there is a treatment and where this treatment can be found. Without these two factors, efforts to make health stations available, for instance, would be useless. But there is also an economic factor: the parents need to be able to afford the treatment.

No matter what we think about the relationship between poverty and child labor, we accept that one of the facilitating elements for the development and public acceptance of an antislavery movement in the United Kingdom and in the northern United States was the changing economic premises for production. Increased industrialization and production methods that were less labor-intensive no doubt "allowed" people to become more critical of slavery—after all, it was no longer crucial to their survival. While we don't think child labor is critical for family survival in most cases, we do realize that the other family members will feel the impact of a sudden reduction of child labor. They will feel it in the sense that the adults may have to work more—and possibly in lower-status activities—and in the sense that the household will have to reduce its consumption.

Contrary to the common perception that poor people really have no choice in how to use their meager income, we think that even relatively poor African families often have some room to maneuver in allocating consumption and expenditures. Research examining spending patterns in African countries indicates, for instance, that there is considerable room for improved consumption planning. As mentioned earlier, in many cases children may be pulled out of school and sent to work in response to a household crisis, while alternative (and seemingly less dramatic) crisis coping mechanisms remain untouched. Among them would be a reduction in parental expenditures for alcohol and clothing.

Even poor families with working children give in to social pressure and may spend amazing amounts of money on traditional ceremonies. And with good reason, from their point of view. Kambili, an agricultural extension agent, explains it very clearly: "You ask me how can it be that I sent my youngest daughter to work to help pay for her grandfather's funeral. If I don't give my father a proper burial, people will think that we are a family good for nothing with no respect for tradition, and no one will want to marry my children. So, what is better for little Sonia: to be educated but covered in shame and without a husband, or to be unable to read and write but respected and married?" Kambili cannot be criticized for wanting what he thought the best for his daughter. What is at issue here is changing what the best can be, and how to obtain it. As long as a family's reputation is more dependent on the amount of alcohol they serve their guests than on having their children schooled, it will be difficult for parents to choose in favor of their children's education when money is tight. Yet this social pressure can and should be addressed, preferably in a participatory manner.

Although there is reason to be extremely cautious with economic transfers, it is clear that certain types of economic assistance to families can do much to reduce child labor. Most important, such transfers need to be well targeted and preferably conditional, since we have learned that a transfer in itself could just as easily lead to increased rather than reduced child labor (see Chapter 1). Surely we also need to avoid the perception that parents should be paid to protect and educate their own children, but there is merit in not forcing parents to make hard decisions. Besides, it is much easier to gain local support for—and participation in—a project that brings more immediate benefits beyond the vague idea of a return in terms of increased support in the future from healthier and more successful children.

Among the most promising interventions are the so-called conditional transfers. The idea is simple. Parents are given a transfer in kind (food, fuel) or cash in exchange for sending children to school instead of work. The best-known example is probably the Brazilian "Bolsa Escola" program, which was launched by the government to get children out of dangerous workplaces. To compensate the family for lost income, a monthly sum roughly equivalent to the child's salary plus school-related expenditures is given to the mother (considered more likely to be a wise manager of the household budget than the father) on condition that the child attends school regularly or has graduated. Bolsa Escola has proven quite effective and similar approaches have been adopted in many Latin American countries as well as elsewhere (Turkey and the West Bank and Gaza), although more often with the explicit goal of keeping children in school rather than reducing harmful child labor.

The problem with conditional transfers is that they have been successfully tested only in middle- and lower-middle-income countries, so their feasibility in the average low-income African country is still to be demonstrated. Certainly the Brazilian approach would have to be adapted to account for much more limited resources in the African context. For example, the construction of basic community infrastructure, such as village wells or pumps, could be conditioned by a contract whereby parents commit to send children to school instead of giving them new labor tasks to replace water fetching. To simplify administrative arrangements, poor families could be given a small grant when children graduate from the third, fifth, and sixth grades. This arrangement may not address the concerns of the poorest families, who will need to make up for a child's lost income, but in a way it is qualitatively superior to simply supporting families who send their children to school, since graduation also presupposes time and conditions for children to do homework and attend classes regularly, and probably for parents to provide support and motivation. Another type of conditional transfer that aims to increase enrollment of at-risk children is a proposal being tested in Swaziland: schools will be rewarded based on the number of vulnerable children they manage to get to attend school on a regular basis. It is important to stress that economic incentives will not change the way people think about child labor and education, so they do not replace IEC/CBC projects. The need to comprehend and internalize *why* child labor is undesirable for children, families, and communities remains a prerequisite for any intervention with long-term ambitions.

Step 2: Legal Reforms

Unfortunately, legislation geared at eliminating child labor is like offering a starving child a slice of imaginary cake. International laws are not enforceable, so that even though a country may become a signatory to a UN convention that protects children from work, these laws become little more than window dressing for debt-ridden countries eager to please Westerns donors.[2]

Is there a point in creating new laws in a country that has few, if any, resources to disseminate and enforce its current laws? Is legislation an effective means to combat child labor in Africa? Opinions are strong, both for and against, but one thing is certain: it is difficult to measure the effect of the introduction of a child labor law in most African countries. The social traditions tend to be much stronger than the judicial systems, and the expectations for enforcement of such "soft" laws are typically even weaker than in the legislative systems themselves.

So why bother? Enormous resources have gone into the processes of developing and ratifying international charters, declarations, and conventions, and later to have these texts incorporated into national legislation. Did they make a difference to most working children in Africa? How many children have the police rescued from exploitative workplaces? How many employers have been prosecuted and penalized for having unduly exploited the labor of a child? Child labor laws may not be particularly effective in deterring individuals from exploiting children, but they are likely to have an important function by establishing a *normative standard* in a society. Universal education is a good example. When laws to that effect were first passed in the Western world, many criticized them for setting impossible standards. But having universal education as a sanctioned goal prompted the adoption of a number of policies that in the end resulted in full enrollment rates. One may argue that what made the difference was an improvement in the living conditions of the masses and changes in the mode of production, but it is hard to believe that economic factors alone provide an explanation. All societies need normative standards, not to produce overnight changes—as the critics rightfully deem impossible—but to set a mark for where society should be, and therefore indicate the direction toward which collective behavior should head. Without such clearly identified standards, social policy would probably content itself with a series of Band-Aid approaches, trying to mend what seems wrong rather than striving to prevent it from happening in the first place.

Overall, the share of resources spent on creating legal texts and frameworks is much larger than the share spent to obtain local inputs and support the application of newly created laws and regulations. But centrally defined and imposed laws are incomprehensible to many common citizens, often because they stem from charters and conventions developed in cultures and ideological systems far from their local reality.[3] In a democratic society, laws need to generally reflect people's perception of justice. Laws that don't are likely to have very little impact, and may even be perceived as so provocative that they instead strengthen subcultures of alternative normative systems in a joint front against foreign and unrecognizable values. Thus, for people to contribute to moving society toward a goal (in our case, the elimination of harmful child labor), they need to agree that this goal is a worthy cause to strive for. Just as IEC projects can help people understand and internalize a new standard, if such projects give people a channel to influence and adjust this standard to reflect the local sense of justice, the same is true for legal frameworks: they may help change normative standards and behaviors, but they need to seek local feedback and take it into consideration. This is particularly so in countries characterized by widespread illiteracy, poor access to communication, limited public outreach, and a general distrust for the central government and its police and court systems.

Legislating child labor in Africa is greatly complicated by the fact that only a marginal share of child laborers work in the formal sector and most child labor is unpaid family help. Compared to Asia and Latin America, largely rural and unindustrialized Africa offers few formal workplaces to be regulated and even fewer labor contracts to be modified. In order to effectively target child labor, legislation would thus need to approach the sensitive relationships within families. More precisely, it will need to challenge the traditional authority and rights that parents have over their children. Given the overwhelming practical and ideological implications for the enforcement of such laws, it seems more practical to suggest a law imposing compulsory schooling than to legislate the active prohibition of full-time work.[4]

In the case of the relatively few children found in the worst forms of child labor, the situation is obviously different, and it becomes crucial for legislators to identify and define this group well. For instance, it may be good for fundraising and newspaper headlines to label all West African child labor migrants as victims of trafficking. However, as pointed out by Sarah Castle and Aisse Diarra, stigmatizing them all as victims and criminalizing their helpers as intermediaries can have dramatic and unwanted consequences.[5] With regard to the "real" trafficking victims, most notably in the sex industry, it must on the other side be a priority for both national and international law enforcement bodies to systematically convict the individuals who profit. Similarly, clear laws must allow for the necessary prosecution of companies that profit either directly or indirectly from exploiting children in mines or similarly detrimental activities.

Having mentioned both intranational and supranational laws and conventions, we should not forget a less applied legal tool: extranational legislation. This type of legislation is applied not in the country where the child was born or works but in a third country, in this context nor-

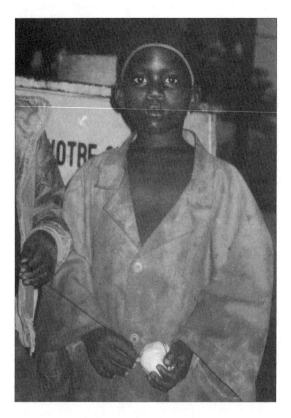

Legislation is less likely to be an efficient tool on a continent where the majority of child labor is family controlled. The very worst forms of child labor abuse, however, need to be clearly identified and defined, and people who profit systematically from such abuse need to be held responsible and given harsh sentences.

mally a country that imports products that may have been produced with the input of economically exploited children. There has been a series of more or less effective unofficial boycotts of child-produced goods in several Western countries—most well known is perhaps the boycott of certain handmade carpets from Central Asia. Official US law, however, prohibits the import of goods produced by laborers working under slaverylike conditions, including abusive child labor. This law has come to gain significance in the case of foreign child workers on West African cocoa farms.[6] As a pioneer, the international cocoa industry has contributed to establishing a broad-based coalition aimed at "cleaning up" the sector, which has spurred a range of initiatives in the countries involved in cocoa farming. It is too early to judge the extent to which this US import law can contribute to reducing rates of harmful child labor, but it is tempting to speculate that without it the cocoa industry would have been considerably less inclined to finance research and activities for child protection in cocoa-growing areas.

Step 3: Enforcement and Coping

Like it or not, cost-effectiveness must be a key concern when it comes to recommending interventions against harmful child labor. It is all the more key in Africa, where severe resource limitations and the weak implementation capacity of most countries demand the selection of only a few priorities for action. So the question is: How can each dollar help as many children as possible maximize their potential or at least prevent developmental harm? Organizing rescue efforts for the rehabilitation of children who have ended up in the most terrible situations may be emotionally gratifying but certainly less cost-effective than concentrating on less dramatic preventive action. It should be safe to say that the price of fully rehabilitating a child soldier—to the extent that this is even possible—would be equivalent to the cost of preventing perhaps a hundred other children from ending up in a similar situation. While experiencing the satisfaction of their happiness and progress, we'd have to close our eyes to the fact that a thousand more child soldiers stand behind us in the streets and that the number of new recruits keeps rising. This practical and ethical dilemma is at the core of policymaking. Although realizing that prevention may be more cost-effective, how can we, as human beings, *not* try to help children in heart-wrenching conditions? All those working with children in difficult situations have to face this question and search for an equilibrium between heart and mind. Each government, each NGO, each donor, and each individual must find their own answer.

Sometimes heart and mind pull in the same direction, because investing in the rescue and rehabilitation of seriously harmed children may actually be cost-effective. This is when the societal costs of nonintervention are so high that the individual cost of rehabilitating the children, though still high in itself, pales in comparison. Take the example of street children. Interventions to rescue them and turn them into law-abiding and productive citizens are among the most expensive on a per capita basis. Yet the cost of nonaction can be extremely high in terms of increased insecurity, lost business, lost investments, property damage, and a greater burden on the police, health, and judicial systems. Moreover, ignoring the extreme misery of some children—or living in a community that does—is likely to affect average citizens. As people, it dehumanizes us in a way that may have a substantial, although hard-to-measure impact on our self-esteem and behavior, as well as on the social capital of our community. And social capital, in turn, has been shown to have a positive impact on economic development and democratic stability.[7] Societies and communities that ignore their weakest members on the basis of a practical or economic argument may thus lose much more than what they save.

The common argument for rescue-type actions is that legal efforts and long-term attitude change through IEC projects tend to be of little help to the children who are already overworked or exploited in Africa. However, effectively helping them can be difficult. Because the children in the most hazardous forms of child labor are often manipulated into a state of acceptance of their situation, many aid workers have found it hard to help individual children understand why he or she needs to be rescued or rehabilitated in the first place. We have mentioned that children intercepted in the course of trafficking from Benin tend to be upset at the prospect of being returned to their families. Girls rescued from even the most horrible brothels have at times escaped their rescuers and fled back into their misery.[8] Street children and child soldiers have often, at some level, taught themselves to enjoy their situations of assumed freedom and power, respectively. To understand this, one must try to comprehend how enslavement in many situations is foremost about the enslavement of the mind. Freeing a child, therefore, may require more than physically removing him or her from the situation of abuse: it may require a transformation of the child's psyche. While some children will welcome the rescuer with open arms, the hard cases will refuse to be helped, defend their exploiter, and in some instances even need to be imprisoned in order not to return to their original situation of abuse.

The need to work *with* the child, with his or her acceptance, and with respect for him or her, requires highly qualified personnel and great patience. If at all possible, the children's transfer out of their situations of abuse should be gradual. Counseling may be the most efficient way to empower and prepare children in exploitative situations to take charge of their future life choices and prevent continued long-term abuse. If children can be helped to develop their own motivation to change their life, improvements are likely to be more sustainable, because children will be committed to them.

Rescue operations can be very complex in at least two ways. First, the rescuer must be prepared to take the responsibility for the children rescued, with all that is involved. Sometimes this turns out to be both more costly and more difficult than anticipated. For instance, the child's parents may turn out to be unsuitable for reunification efforts, or the child may turn out to have developed conditions, such as HIV or severe psychiatric disorders, that demand great resources to be dealt with. Second, rehabilitation and reinsertion require long-term follow-up, which is both costly and difficult. Not coincidentally, this is one of the most common weaknesses of many current projects. For example, evaluating a recent Benin reinsertion project for children who had been intercepted during trafficking, the project team found that 80 percent of the children had been retrafficked. Enormous amounts of money tend to be wasted because not enough attention is paid to follow-up, thus jeopardizing sustainability.[9]

The prospects for "rescued" children are typically not good, especially in the long run, and evaluation reports have yet to identify the "right" approach to rehabilitation. The only element that seems to be a common denominator for successful projects is to have highly committed people involved—corny as it may sound, love is the only silver bullet we know of. A good project worker is available to the traumatized child on the child's own premises, preferably twenty-four hours a day and over a period of several years, and he or she feels a profound commitment to protecting and rebuilding the dignity of the child. The love of project workers cannot be bought with money. But at least good project administrators may spend more time identifying and recruiting the right people, and then support them so that they don't burn out and lose the love and idealism with which they often begin their career.

8

Conclusion

THE DISCUSSION HAS TAKEN US TO THE HOUR WHEN MOSQUITOES REALLY start biting, and chatting in the shade of the large mango tree is no longer pleasant. It's time to wrap up and go, our friends back to their families and us back to the hotel. We have talked about the forms of child labor and the damage they can do, but we have had little time to ponder their causes and what can be done about them. Perhaps we could do that some other time? The answer comes in a kind but resigned tone, as if in fear of disappointing us, well-meaning foreigners, with an obvious truth: "Look, Africa is such a poor continent with so many problems—of course we have child labor. It may be terrible, but it's unavoidable. How would you even start to do something about it in this context?"

We have met this sort of fatalistic attitude so many times that we are hardly surprised. And it's not just Africans. People from richer countries often show a similar defeatism, but put a historical spin on it: "When we were that poor, we also used child labor. So why wouldn't Africa?"

It is this willingness to accept the suffering and stunted development of millions of African children *as inevitable* that prompted us to write this book. We wanted to show that even though not all work is bad for children, some of it might be very harmful. Not just to children, but to society as a whole. More than anything else, we wanted to show that it doesn't have to be this way, despite poverty and other difficulties. There are, in fact, things that can be done to make the situation better: we simply cannot afford to wait until Africa becomes as wealthy as Europe and hope that the problem will solve itself.

We've tried to debunk the myth that many African children must work because their families are too poor. Empirical studies show that the relationship between child labor and poverty is far from straightforward; therefore, a moderate wealth increase would not have any substantial impact on the child labor situation in Africa, at least not in the short run. At any rate, even if child labor were a natural part of poverty, there would be no reason for inaction because the exploitation of children undermines the very economic development that would eventually result in the elimination of child labor. Although it is true—and perhaps even understandable—that abuse of children happens more frequently in poor households worldwide due to the stress that is often related to poverty,[1] by no means does this make it more acceptable.

Something to keep in mind is that the priority given to children varies greatly *among* the poor. The distribution of nutritious food among household members is perhaps the best illustration of this variation. Some poor households will make sure that children get the food necessary to grow up healthy, too bad if it means that the adults will have to go hungry. Others will have a rigid pecking order, with men eating first—and to their satisfaction—and children eating last, whatever is left.[2]

Similarly, time allocation data show that the labor burden within households tends to be quite unevenly distributed and in most places men work less than women.[3] It stands to reason that if some men had worked as much as their spouses, their children might have had less work to do and more time for studying or playing. Thus it is also a questionable argument to say that child labor is inevitable because there is simply too much work to do in the typical African household.

These priority differences among poor populations are related to traditional cultural norms on one hand, and the development of individualism and social disintegration on the other. The founder of the Grameen Bank, Mohammed Yunus, has stated that finding ways to carry the burdens of poverty with dignity should be a primary objective.[4] Maintaining high standards for self-respect and interpersonal behavior will probably, in turn, support development and economic growth. Respecting the integrity and value of children is among the most elementary of such standards.

As for the historical argument of many Westerners (and a good number of African intellectuals), it seems to derive from the perception that development is linear, and therefore Africa has to go through more or less the same processes as did Western economies in order to reach a "Western" standard of living. This reasoning forgets that in today's globalized world, less developed countries are no longer condemned to follow their own path of trial and error, because widespread access to knowledge makes it possible to leapfrog to modern technologies and modes of production, and to learn from the mistakes of others even if they are half a world away. No one would expect African countries to rely on typewriters and telexes rather than computers and emails just because Africa is poorer than the West, so why would it be more justifiable for Africa to impose excessive labor burdens on children? Also, circumstances are simply not similar enough to the more ignorant times when child exploitation was commonplace in Western countries, because now we know better how harmful it is.

Promoting anti–child labor programs in Africa today is often perceived as some sort of cultural imperialism, an attempt to transfer cultural values that have no natural place in African societies. It should not be. Child labor should be reduced in Africa today because it interferes with good child development and jeopardizes economic growth. Regardless of culture, most people share the desire to raise smart and strong children who will turn into successful and responsible adults, and that is what this debate should be about. Integration of knowledge does not necessarily require dramatic cultural change. The same way that scientific knowledge has prompted behavioral changes in other cultures, knowledge about the effects of child labor can adjust behavior also in the African countries, within the framework of the local cultures. We know enough about the consequences of child labor today to know that we should not only reduce the suffering of many African children, but also diminish considerable and unnecessary human and social capital losses. It is the responsibility of African leaders to reach out for this knowledge, and it is the responsibility for those with the expertise to share it.

Endnotes

Chapter 1

1. See ILO/SIMPOC 2002.
2. See ibid. and ILO/IPEC 2004.
3. See Reynolds 1991.
4. See Draper 1988.
5. It should be noted, however, that Hazda children have been found to contribute more in the hunting and gathering process. See Blurton Jones 1988.
6. Bush girls played for 44 percent of the observation time and bush boys for 42 percent. Sedentary girls only played for 18 percent of observation time, while sedentary boys played more than bush boys, at 58 percent of observation time.
7. It should suffice to read African literature, for instance Achebe 1994, to find descriptions of this.
8. For more detail on these influences, see Bass 2004 on the cultural and historical context of child labor.
9. See Oloko 1996.
10. See Cockburn 2000 and Nkamleu and Kielland 2004.
11. See ILO/IPEC 2004.
12. While an urban schoolgirl works an average of five and a half hours daily, including schoolwork, her peer who is not in school works more than eight hours. The difference is even more considerable for boys: an urban schoolboy works for four and a half hours daily, while his peer who is not in school also works for more than eight hours.
13. See World Bank 1998.
14. See, for instance, Jensen and Skyt-Nielsen 1997, Canagarajah and Coloumbe 1997, Bhalotra and Heady 2001b, and Bhalotra and Tzannatos 2003, the last of which presents an extensive methodological discussion of these findings.

15. See Deheija and Gatti 2001.

16. However, when controlling the result for another wealth indicator, household consumption, she finds that the child labor–increasing effect from landholding only remains significant for girls' labor. She statistically proves that both girls' participation rate and the hours worked by farming girls increase with the numbers of acres of the household farms, while boys remain less affected. See Bhalotra and Heady 2001a.

17. See Ranjan 2001, Deheija and Gatti 2001, and Jafarey and Lahirib 2002.

18. See Bhalotra and Heady 2001b and Bhalotra and Tzannatos 2003.

19. See Rogers and Swinnerton 2002a.

20. See Jensen and Skyt-Nielsen 1997.

21. Author unknown, "Social, Economic, and Demographic Determinants of Child Labor in Northern Sudan," based on the 1996 migration and labor force survey conducted by the Ministry of Manpower.

22. Some writers argue that male farmers, and particularly cash crop farmers, have a stronger claim on family labor during the farming season, while women tend to control children's labor in everyday life.

23. See Reynolds 1991.

24. See Bradley 1993.

25. See Mueller 1984.

26. See Bass 2004.

27. See Reynolds 1991.

28. The South African nongovernmental organization Molo Songololo writes in its report on trafficking of children for sexual exploitation that children are forced into prostitution to pay debt or to pay for the upkeep of one family member or an entire family, or are sold to provide a dowry. Referring to child prostitution, the report explicitly stresses that "parents, *particularly mothers,* are involved in a number of ways." See Molo Songololo 2000.

29. See, for instance, Case, Paxson, and Ableidinger 2002 and Case and Paxson 2001, which conclude that household expenditure on child-related goods—in particular on healthy foods—is lower when a child's biological mother is absent.

30. Case, Paxson, and Ableidinger 2002 concludes that losing a mother has a stronger negative effect on school attendance than losing a father.

31. See Bozari 2003.

32. In the francophone literature, "placing" a child is generally perceived as less committing than "entrusting" a child, the latter assuming a closer relationship between the two families and better care for the child. Entrusting a child will again be less permanent than adoption, while child placement often is an open-ended arrangement.

33. See Isiugo-Abanihe 1985.

34. See Bozari 2003.

35. Data from Macro International survey results for Benin, Cameroon, the Central African Republic, Chad, Comoros, Eritrea, Ethiopia, Gabon, Ghana, Guinea, Kenya, Madagascar, Malawi, Mali, Mauritania, Mozambique, Namibia, Niger, Nigeria, Rwanda, South Africa, Tanzania, Togo, Uganda, Zambia, and Zimbabwe.

36. An exception to this is boys in some rural areas, who are frequently sent to stay with a nearby relative to be able to continue schooling.

37. Case, Paxson, and Ableidinger 2002 shows that this tendency is particularly significant in Tanzania and Ghana, where the presence of an orphan in the household increases the school participation of coresiding nonorphans by 4–5 percent, while the same effect is significant but somewhat smaller in Malawi, Niger, Uganda, and Zambia. The research results have been controlled for other household variables.

38. As a curiosity, Pamela Reynolds also describes child-initiated movements in which children are allowed to move relatively freely within the village community in rural Zimbabwe. See Reynolds 1991.

39. See Akresh 2003.

40. In northern Nigeria an extreme case of family coercion is reported: we find family-initiated practices of mutual fostering between cospouses that are intended to ensure peace and quiet between the various wives in a polygamous family.

41. We found this when analyzing data from a 2000 household survey undertaken by Macro International and Institut National de la Statistique et de l'Analyse Economique in Burkina Faso.

42. The study points out, however, that placed children who stay in their grandparents' household have a slightly better chance of being sent to school than do children who live with both their parents. In Case, Paxson, and Ableidinger 2002, it is speculated that this may be because migrant parents place their children temporarily with grandparents while continuing to support them by transfers.

43. Benin is probably an extreme case, in particular considering its relatively low AIDS rate (5 percent). Almost one-third of children ages 6 to 14 who live in urban areas do not live with either one of their parents, and the vast majority of these children are girls. Presumably, they are mostly placed children, but "placed" for what purpose? The picture coming out of the statistics is what anyone living in Cotonou can confirm: according to Macro International survey data we have analyzed, most of the boys are sent to town to pursue their education (63 percent go to school), while most of the girls are sent to work (only 23 percent go to school).

44. These results stem from our own regression analysis of time allocation data from Benin compiled by the United Nations Development Programme (and a contribution from Niels-Hugo Blunch) (see UNDP 1998). The results we refer to are controlled for age, as one would logically expect that the average age among placed children will be somewhat higher than among children living with their parents, and that older children naturally work more than younger because of their maturity, not because they are placed.

45. Protocol to Prevent, Suppress, and Punish Trafficking in Persons, Especially Women and Children, supplementing the United Nations Convention Against Transnational Organized Crime.

46. Sarah Castle and Aisse Diarra write eloquently about this in the case of what they refer to as "child labor migration" between Mali and Côte d'Ivoire. See Castle and Diarra 2003.

47. The term *transaction* refers to "any institution or practice through which young people, below 18 years of age, are handed over by either or both parents, or by a guardian to a third person, whether for a fee or not, with the intention of exploiting the person or the work of the young person."

48. Perhaps the best example of this type of overzealous cultural sensitivi-

ty is the opposition to efforts to end female genital mutilation, justified by the fact that Westerners are in no position to pass judgment on traditional practices and must respect them.

49. West African child trafficking hit the media headlines a second time in 2001 with a documentary on the use of Malian children on cocoa farms in Côte d'Ivoire. While the *Etireno* case was mainly a humanitarian case, the cocoa case had an economic dimension. Multinational companies were buying the cocoa harvested by children victims of trafficking, and people worldwide ate the chocolate produced using this cocoa.

50. See Kielland and Ouensavi 2001.

51. See Kielland and Sanogo 2002.

52. The United Nations Children's Organization roughly estimates the number of *annual* trafficking cases in the region to be around 200,000, something we find likely to be an overestimation, in particular because not all the child labor migrants in our own surveys strictly qualify as victims of trafficking according to the definitions. See UNICEF 2002.

53. See Castle and Diarra 2003.

54. In a multivariate regression analysis, the household poverty indicator was insignificant for all subsamples. On the other hand, a constructed variable for household wealth relative to average wealth of the households in the same village (a proxy of "perceived" poverty) in fact came out as significant, showing, contrary to the expectations, that households with wealth above the village average are more likely to send children to other countries to work. However, it is important to remember that in rural Africa we tend to talk less about rich and poor, and more about degrees of relative poverty.

55. Around 20 percent of the child labor migrants from Benin had left with a friend, something that is also common in Ghana. Eric Beauchemin reports that children who work in Côte d'Ivoire come home for the celebration of holidays, and that, when they go back, they often take friends or siblings with them. See Beauchemin 1999.

56. Children are often paid in kind. After a season of farm work, the child is sent home with a bicycle or a radio. The admiration of the other children in the village is often enough to ensure easy recruitment for the next season, and the humiliated victims tend to stay quiet about their hardships. It appears that the traffickers are better than the child protection advocates at using the child-to-child method. See Farah 2001.

57. See UNICEF 1999b.

58. This was reported on January 20, 1999, by South Africa's *Sunday Times*.

59. As reported in Molo Songololo 2000.

60. Associazione MAMRE, personal communication, June 2002.

61. See Bales 2000.

62. See Farah 2001.

63. This is a psychological mechanism that resembles what has been called "learned helplessness," the process by which abused women stay with their violent husbands because the continued abuse has made them believe that they deserve the abuse and in any case has rendered them unable to think, let alone fend, for themselves.

64. See UNICEF, UNAIDS, and USAID 2004.

65. Estimates based on data from Macro International survey results for the same countries as cited in endnote 28 above.

66. Case, Paxson, and Ableidinger 2002.

67. This is referred to as the levirate tradition.

68. For example, a study in Uganda found that over one-fourth of AIDS widows had been victims of property grabbing by relatives. A program staff for PLAN International in Tororo reported: "Women . . . are easily sent away from family land by paternal relatives. . . . We have a problem with greed and corruption." See Gilborn et al. 2001.

69. See Rau 2002. See also Nelson Mandela Children's Fund 2001.

70. Preliminary results of an ILO/IPEC rapid assessment on child labor and HIV/AIDS, cited in Rau 2002.

71. A weakness may be that the wealth proxy used is based on a simple six-item index that counts whether the household has a radio, television, refrigerator, bicycle, and car, typically male items that per se do not tell us a lot about whether children's needs are covered, as would a more detailed expenditure measurement. See Case, Paxson, and Ableidinger 2002.

72. They find this after controlling for other household characteristics, like number of household members and age, sex, and education of household head, which in fact seems to take much of the impact away from the wealth measurement.

73. See Case, Paxson, and Ableidinger 2002.

74. See UNICEF 2004, statistical annex 4.

75. While it has been suggested that the poorer the household, the greater the discrimination gap between boys and girls, the research found this not to be true. It has furthermore been assumed that the richer the household, the lesser the discrimination gap between orphans and nonorphans, but this assumption was also proven wrong.

76. Andvig, Canagarajah, and Kielland 2001 estimates that, with 5 million living AIDS orphans, and assuming that half of these children are in age groups capable of working, this represents a potential shift in the child labor supply of 2.5 million. Calculated the same way, the potential child labor supply in Africa is roughly 153.5 million. Very roughly, the number of children actually in the open labor market in sub-Saharan Africa is estimated to be 5 percent—that is, close to 7.7 million (including child domestic servants). Although many of the orphans are likely to be absorbed into the extended family and neighborhood networks, it is clear that the prevalence of AIDS means a considerable supply shift. The family system will be important regarding the effects of the AIDS epidemic on children. While, for example, an effective extended family system may absorb nine-tenths of the children, a disintegrated family system may only be able to handle two-thirds. In the first case, only 250,000 will be left alone to cope, or about 3 percent of the children's labor market; in the last case, more than 830,000, or about 10 percent.

Chapter 2

1. See Kielland and Ouensavi 2001 on Benin, Mueller 1984 on Botswana, Reynolds 1991 on Zimbabwe, Cockburn 2000 on Ethiopia, and Mason and Khandker 1998 on Tanzania. On northern Sudan, we refer to analysis of the 1996 migration and labor force survey conducted by the Ministry of Manpower.

2. See World Bank 1996.

3. See Reynolds 1991.

4. See Tørres 2000.

5. See Mueller 1984.

6. See Cockburn 2000.

7. See Alderman et al. 1995 and Basu and Ray 2002. E. R. Fahopunda argues that the typical African household may not in fact be defined as a household in the first place, since the technical definition of a household assumes income pooling, unambiguous boundaries, and monogamous marriages. See Fahopunda 1978

8. See Balsvik.

9. See Staudt 1987.

10. See Doss 2001.

11. Referred to in Balsvik, with references to Jones 1983 and McKee 1986.

12. It has been argued that African men have the stronger customary claims on the work of other family members, but the argument is far from settled. For example, Christopher Udry found child labor input to be twice as high on men's farms than on women's in his study of six villages in the strongly hierarchical Burkina Faso, but Pamela Reynolds found that 80 percent of children's labor time in Zimbabwe was spent on maternal plots. See Udry 1996 and Reynolds 1991.

13. Perhaps more than anywhere, economic literature on rural household production tends to treat children merely as passive victims of adult decision-making. Few economists have seriously attempted to include children as active participants in the household bargaining model. For an exception, see Iversen 2002.

14. See Reynolds 1991.

15. See Mueller 1984.

16. In general, the more labor required of the mother to take care of her children's basic needs, the greater the responsibility for the older child who remains at home.

17. The demographic figures used here come from Macro International survey results.

18. Time allocation data from UNDP 1998.

19. See Hussmann, Mehran, and Verma 1990.

20. See ILO/SIMPOC 2002.

21. See Mueller 1984.

22. See Teffera and Fisseha 2001.

Chapter 3

1. We make a distinction between apprenticeship and vocational training. The former tends to be less formal and more personalized, with children generally learning by doing in a fairly unstructured environment. The latter implies the existence of some sort of educational facility and a more structured learning environment that combines theory and practice for children grouped in classes. Apprenticeship tends to be more long-term than vocational training (e.g., three

to four years versus one). The apprenticeship described here is more typically western African, while in eastern and southern Africa trades are more often learned through vocational training or through families (e.g., father to son).

2. See Kadonys, Madihi, and Mtwana 2002.

3. See Jekinnou 2002.

4. See Kadonys, Madihi, and Mtwana 2002.

5. See Parikh 2002.

6. Ibid.

7. According to interviews with Roger Ouensavi, former director of the nongovernmental organization Centre d'Ecoute et d'Orientation, whose work involves repatriation of child victims of trafficking in Benin.

8. Our own translation from the French-language novel *L'aventure ambigüe*. See Hamidou Kane 1961.

9. See Amadou and Koto Sero 2001.

10. See UNICEF 1998.

11. A medical examination of 500 randomly selected talibés in the three northern regions of Benin found a malaria incidence of 90 percent and an intestinal parasite incidence of over 85 percent in boys. See Amadou and Koto Sero 2001.

12. Our own translation from the French-language novel *L'aventure ambigüe*. See Hamidou Kane 1961.

13. According to an unofficial report from Creative Associates.

14. See Hunt 1993.

15. See Amadou and Koto Sero 2001.

Chapter 4

1. See Lee Barnes and Boddy 1995.

2. Ibid.

3. See Nchahaga 2002 and Gonza and Moshi 2002.

4. See ILO/IPEC 1997.

5. See Tørres 2000.

6. See Lee Barnes and Boddy 1995.

7. Own analysis of Macro International survey data from Togo (Demographic and Health Survey, 1998).

8. See Andvig, Canagarajah, and Kielland 2001.

9. See Black.

10. See Onyango 1991a.

11. See Lee Barnes and Boddy 1995.

12. For example, in a sample of women in their 30s, 40s, and 50s in Lagos, two out of three replied that they had been involved in street trade as children. See Oloko 1996.

13. Children's contributions are particularly important in the case of Muslim women who are not allowed to leave their houses, as their commerce activity is possible only through the use of the household's children (including child domestics), or through the services of neighborhood children.

14. The richest quintile, on the other hand, employed significantly fewer

children, probably because they could afford more skilled adult labor. Based on our own analysis of Macro International survey data.

15. See Oloko 1996.
16. See Beauchemin 1999.
17. See Lee Barnes and Boddy 1995.
18. See Abalo 1992.
19. See Agarwal et al. 1994.
20. See Beauchemin 1999.
21. See Lee Barnes and Boddy 1995.

Chapter 5

1. See ILO 1996b.
2. See ILO/SIMPOC 2002.
3. See Walker 1998. The forced marriage of widows to brothers-in-law, called levirate, is a tradition practiced by many African ethnic groups.
4. See Kadonys, Madihi, and Mtwana 2002.
5. In Tanzanian quarries, typhoid was also found. See Kadonys, Madihi, and Mtwana 2002.
6. See Junger 2000.
7. See Kpoghomou 1996.
8. See Mwami, Sanga, and Nyoni 2002.
9. Other common diseases are tuberculosis, diarrhea, and respiratory infections. There are also risks of injury due to irresponsible use of explosives, children falling into mining holes (which can be up to 60 meters deep), and ceilings collapsing inside the corridors of mines. In Tanzania it is also pointed out that child miners are exposed to mercury, possibly leading to long-term health and neurological problems. See Mwami, Sanga, and Nyoni 2002.
10. Our own translation from Bruyère 2001.
11. See Tovo 1995.
12. See, for example, Frase-Blunt 2002.
13. See Molo Songololo 2000.
14. See Kamala et al. 2001.
15. See ILO/SIMPOC 2002.
16. See Coalition to Stop the Use of Child Soldiers, Africa report.
17. See Machel 1997.
18. See Richards, et al. 2003.
19. Graça Machel reports: "One of the common tasks assigned to children is to serve as porters, often carrying very heavy loads of up to 60 kilograms including ammunition or injured soldiers. Children who are too weak to carry their loads are liable to be savagely beaten or even shot." See Machel 1997.
20. See Coalition to Stop the Use of Child Soldiers, Africa report.
21. See, for example, Richards et al. 2003.
22. Ibid.
23. See Beauchemin 1999.
24. In Beauchemin's report, 82 percent of the schoolchildren interviewed said that they would like to leave their village. See Beauchemin 1999.

25. See the particularly rich bibliography in Marguerat 2001.
26. See Beauchemin 1999.

Chapter 6

1. See Miller 1997.
2. See Mwami, Sanga, and Nyoni 2002.
3. See International Institute of Tropical Agriculture 2002.
4. Ibid.
5. Anthropologists have been studying and comparing the psychosocial consequences of children's work, and there is considerable evidence suggesting that the amount and type of work in which the children are involved has an impact on their overall behavior and personality. For example, children frequently involved in domestic and subsistence activities have been found to develop patterns of social interaction that are more efficient and purposeful than those of other children, and girls put in charge of younger siblings have been found to behave in a nurturing fashion in general. See Munroe, Munroe, and Shimmin 1984.
6. See, for example, Wenger 1989, a study on Kenya's children. See also the seminal work Whiting and Whiting 1975.
7. See, for instance, Belsky 1993.
8. See UNICEF 2002.
9. See Blaauw 2002.
10. See Agossou 2000.
11. See Balier 1994.
12. See Becker 2001.
13. See OMCT 2001.
14. See Agossou 2000.
15. See, for instance, Menic, "Les enfants victimes d'abus sexuels en Afrique ou l'imbroglio d'un double paradoxe: L'exemple du Cameroun"; Seignon, "L'exploitation sexuelle et la prostitution des mineurs en République du Bénin"; Seck, "Les abus sexuels au Sénégal," in Agossou 2000.
16. De Souza 2000.
17. See Seignon, "L'exploitation sexuelle et la prostitution des mineurs en République du Bénin," in Agossou 2000.
18. See Machel 1997.
19. See Amnesty International 2000.
20. Ibid.
21. See Human Rights Watch Africa 1997.
22. See World Bank 1998.
23. Nkamleu and Kielland 2004.
24. See Akabayashi and Psacharopoulos 1999.
25. See Heady 2003.
26. See Sall 2000.
27. Thus in Figure 6.2, the money the child earns at age 7 has its real value, but the money he or she earns at age 8 has its value minus 5 percent, correcting for the loss of interest in the year of investment. The money the child earns at age 9 has its value minus 5 percent for the first year, and an additional 5 percent for the second year, and so on.

28 See ILO/IPEC 2004. The ILO estimates a return of seven dollars to each dollar invested in eradicating child labor and placing children in school.

Chapter 7

1. The opposite is also true: laws tend to be modified to reflect a change in commonly accepted behavior only when the distance between the two is not very large.

2. See Bass 2004.

3. It is not surprising that African families tend to settle issues between themselves on their own or with the help of traditional leaders, rather than involving the police and court systems, which are alien institutions in most traditional communities.

4. See Basu and Van 1999.

5. See Castle and Diarra 2003.

6. To learn more, see the so-called Harkin-Engels Protocol, which was signed by representatives of the cocoa industry, labor unions (including the ILO), and civil society organizations (including Free the Slaves). Available online at http://www.responsiblecocoa.org/pdfs/protocol-english.pdf.

7. See, for instance, Inglehart 1997.

8. See, for instance, Bales 2000.

9. Personal communication with Roger Ouensavi, director of the Centre d'Ecoute et d'Orientation, a shelter for child victims of traffic.

Chapter 8

1. See Belsky 1993.

2. In Niger, one of Africa's poorest countries, we heard a counterargument that is not completely invalid. A seasoned pediatrician suggested that when parents eat the only nutritious food available, this could actually represent the best survival strategy for children: if the parents were to starve to death, young children would surely also die. This explanation, however, would be legitimate only in extreme—and therefore rare—cases.

3. For comparisons of men's and women's workdays, see, for instance, Mueller 1994 or Brown and Haddad 1994 on Botswana; Saito, Mekonnen, and Spurling 1994 on Burkina Faso, Kenya, Nigeria, and Zambia; BDPA on the Central African Republic; Bério 1984 on Côte d'Ivoire; Kamuzora 1980 on Tanzania; and UNDP 1998 on Benin. Without having the data too prove it, we suspect also that many women prefer to use their own or others' children as aids rather than working more themselves, even when this means that the children will not be able to go to school or do their homework properly.

4. The Grameen Bank is a microcredit methodology for the very poorest that was developed in Bangladesh and later applied around the world. It is widely acknowledged as one of the most successful approaches for delivering people out of absolute poverty.

References

Abalo, Essodina M. 1992. "Analyse descriptive du phénomène des jeunes filles en situation difficile dans la ville de Lomé." Mimeograph. UNICEF.

Abidoye, G. 1997. "Children at Work: A Study on Child Labour in Nigeria." Paper presented at the Conference on Urban Childhood, Trondheim, June.

Achebe, C. 1994. *Things Fall Apart.* New York: Anchor Books.

Adepoju, A., and C. Oppong. 1994. *Gender, Work, and Population in Sub-Saharan Africa.* London: ILO.

Adihou, F. A., and N. Fanou-Ako. 1998. "Le trafic des enfants entre le Bénin et le Gabon." Research report. Anti-Slavery International and Enfants Solidares d'Afrique et du Monde. Benin.

Agarwal, B. 1997. "Bargaining and Gender Relations: Within and Beyond the Household." *Feminist Economics* 3: 1–51.

Agarwal, S., M. Attah, N. Apt, M. Grieco, E. A. Kwakye, and J. Turner. 1994. "Bearing the Weight: The Kayayoo, Ghana's Working Girl Child." Paper presented at a UNICEF conference, Delhi, February.

Agossou, T. 2000. *Regards d'Afrique sur la Maltraitance.* Paris: Editions Karthala.

Ainsworth, M. 1996. "Economic Aspects of Child Fostering in the Ivory Coast." *Research in Population Economics:* 25–62.

Akabayashi, H., and G. Psacharopoulos. 1999. "The Trade-Off Between Child Labor and Human Capital Formation: A Tanzanian Case Study." *Journal of Development Studies* 35, no. 5.

Akresh, R. 2003. "Risk, Network Quality, and Family Structure: Child Fostering Decisions in Burkina Faso." Yale University, Department of Economics.

Alderman, H., P. A. Chiappori, L. Haddad, J. Hoddinott, and R. Kanbur. 1995. "Unitary vs. Collective Models of the Household: Is It Time to Shift the Burden of Proof?" *World Bank Research Observer* 10: 1–19.

Amadou, M., and S. Koto Sero. 2001. "Les talibés au Nord Bénin: Enfance Melheureuse—Un mode de vie choisi." NGO report. PIED Benin.

Amnesty International. 2000. *Hidden Scandal, Secret Shame: Torture and Ill-Treatment of Children*. London.

Andvig, J. C. 1997. "Child Labor in Sub-Saharan Africa: An Exploration." Oslo: Norwegian Institute of International Affairs.

———. 2001. "Family-Controlled Child Labor in Sub-Saharan Africa: A Survey of Research." World Bank Social Protection Discussion Paper no. 0122.

———. 2002 "An Essay on Child Labor in Sub-Saharan Africa: A Bargaining Approach."

Andvig, J. C., S. Canagarajah, and A. Kielland. 2001. "Issues in Child Labor in Africa." World Bank Africa Region Human Development Working Paper Series.

Ashagrie, K. 1993. "Statistics on Child Labor: A Brief Report." *Bulletin of Labour Statistics* 3: 11–28.

Baland, J. M., and J. A. Robinson. 2000. "Is Child Labor Inefficient?" *Journal of Political Economy:* 663–679.

———. 2002. "Rotten Parents." *Journal of Public Economics*.

Bales, K. 2000. *Disposable People: New Slavery in the Global Economy*. University of California Press.

Balier, C. 1994. "L'inceste: Un meurtre d'identité." *Psychiatrie de l'Enfant* 37, no. 2.

Balsvik, R. "Intra Household Bargaining with Commitment Problems: Consequences for Productive Efficiency." University of Oslo, Department of Economics.

Bass, L. E. 2004. *Child Labor in Sub-Saharan Africa*. Boulder: Lynne Rienner.

Basu, K. 1999. "Child Labor: Cause, Consequence, and Cure, with Remarks on International Labor Standards." *Journal of Economic Literature:* 1083–1119.

———. 2002. "A Note on Multiple General Equilibria with Child Labor." *Economics Letters*.

Basu, K., and R. Ray. 2002. "The Collective Model of the Household and an Unexpected Implication for Child Labor." World Bank Policy Research Working Paper no. 2813.

Basu, K., and P. H. Van. 1998. "The Economics of Child Labor." *American Economic Review* 88, no. 3: 412–427.

———. 1999. "The Economics of Child Labor: Reply." *American Economic Review* 89, no. 5: 1386–1388.

Beauchemin, E. 1999. "The Exodus: The Growing Migration of Children from Ghana's Rural Areas to the Urban Centers." Catholic Action for Street Children and UNICEF.

Becker, J. 2001. "Easy Targets: Violence Against Children World Wide." *Human Rights Watch:* 36.

Bekombo, M. 1981. "The Child in Africa: Socialisation, Education, and Work." In *Child Work, Poverty, and Underdevelopment*, eds. G. Rodgers and G. Standing. Geneva: ILO.

Belle, D., ed. 1989. *Children's Social Networks and Supports*. New York: John Wiley and Sons.

Belsky, J. 1993. "The Etiology of Child Maltreatment: A Developmental–Ecological Analysis." *Psychological Bulletin* 114, no. 3: 413–434.

Bério, A. J. 1984. "The Analysis of Time Allocation and Activity Patterns in

Nutrition and Rural Development Planning." *Food and Nutrition Bulletin* 6, no. 1.

Bhalotra, S., and C. Heady. 2001a. "Child Farm Labor: The Wealth Paradox." World Bank Social Protection Discussion Paper no. 0125.

———. 2001b. "Determinants of Child Farm Labor in Ghana and Pakistan: A Comparative Study." Department for International Development, Employment and Labor Markets Program.

Bhalotra, S., and Z. Tzannatos. 2003. "Child Labor: What Have We Learned?" World Bank Social Protection Discussion Paper no. 0317.

Blaauw, M. 2002. *Sexual Torture of Children: An Ignored and Concealed Crime.*

Black, M. *Child Domestic Workers: A Handbook for Research and Action.* Anti-Slavery International's Child Labor Series no. 15.

Bledsoe, C. 1994. "Children Are Like Young Bamboo Trees: Potentiality and Reproduction in Sub-Saharan Africa." In *Population, Economic Development, and the Environment,* eds. K. Lindahl-Kiessling and H. Landberg. Oxford University Press.

Blunch, N., S. Canagarajah, and S. Goyal. 2002. "Short and Long Term Impact of Economic Policies on Child Labor and Schooling in Ghana." World Bank Social Protection Discussion Paper no. 0212.

Blunch, N., A. Dar, L. Guarcello, S. Lyon, A. Ritualo, and F. Rosati. 2002. "Child Work in Zambia: A Comparative Study of Survey Instruments." World Bank Social Protection Discussion Paper no. 0228.

Blunch, N., A. Dar, and B. Kim. 2002. "Participation of Children in Schooling and Labor Activities: A Review of Empirical Studies." World Bank Social Protection Discussion Paper no. 0221.

Blunch, N., and D. Verner. 2000. "Revisiting the Link Between Poverty and Child Labor: The Ghanaian Experience." World Bank Policy Research Working Paper no. 2488.

Blurton Jones, N. G. 1988. *Measuring and Modeling Costs of Children in Two Foraging Societies: Comparative Sociology of Mammals and Man.* Eds. R. Fley and V. Standen.

Blyth Whiting, B. 1996. "The Effect of Social Change on Concepts of the Good Child and Good Mothering: A Study of Families in Kenya." *Ethos* 24, no. 1: 3–35.

Boonpala, P., and J. Kane. 2001. "Trafficking of Children: The Problem and Responses Worldwide." ILO/IPEC.

Boserup, E. 1970. *Woman's Role in Economic Development.* New York: Allen and Unwin.

Bozari, M. 2003. *Le rôle des enfants dans les stratégies de gestion du risque au sein des ménages au Niger.* UNICEF/Ministère du Développement Social, de la Promotion de la Femme, de la Protection de l'Enfant.

Bradley, Candice. 1993. "Women's Power, Children's Labor." *Cross-Cultural Research* 27, nos 1–2: 70–96.

Brown, L., and L. Haddad. 1994. "Time Allocation Patterns and Time Burdens: A Gender Analysis of Seven Countries." Washington, D.C.: International Food Policy Research Institute.

Bruyère, Jean-Michel, ed. 2001. *L'envers du jour: Mondes réels et imaginaires des enfants errants de Dakar.* Paris: Léo Scheer.

Bryceson, D. F., ed. 1995. *Women Wielding the Hoe.* Oxford: Berg.

Bwibo, N., and P. Onyango. 1987. "Final Report of Child Labour and Health Research." Report to the World Health Organization, Nairobi.

Caldwell, J. C., et al. 1992. "A New Type of Fertility Transition in Africa." *Population and Development Review:* 211–242.

Canagarajah, S., and H. Coulombe. 1997. "Child Labor and Schooling in Ghana." World Bank Policy Research Working Paper no. 1844.

Canagarajah, S., and H. Skyt-Nielsen. "Child Labor in Africa: A Comparative Study." World Bank/Institute for Economics, Aarhus School of Business.

Case, A., C. Paxson, and J. Ableidinger. 2002. *Orphans in Africa.* Princeton University, Center for Health and Wellbeing, Research Program in Development Studies.

Castle, S., and A. Diarra. 2003. *The International Migration of Young Malians: Tradition, Necessity, or Rite of Passage?* London School of Hygiene and Tropical Medicine.

Cigno, A., F. Rosati, and Z. Tzannatos. 2002. "Child Labor Handbook." World Bank Social Protection Working Paper no. 0206.

Clay, D. C., T. Kampayana, and J. Kayitsinga. "Inequality and the Emergence of Non-Farm Employment in Rwanda." US Agency for International Development.

Cockburn, J. 2000. "Child Labor Versus Education: Poverty Constraints or Income Opportunities?" Oxford University, Center for the Study of African Economics.

Coulombe, H. 1998. "Child Labor and Education in Côte d'Ivoire." Unpublished paper for the World Bank.

Dasgupta, P. 1993. *An Inquiry into Well-Being and Destitution.* Oxford: Clarendon Press.

De Souza, M. 2000. Unpublished study based on interviews with 200 prostitutes in Cotonou and Ouidah.

Deb, P., and F. Rosati. 2002. "Determinants of Child Labor and School Attendance: The Role of Unobservables." Paper presented at the World Bank Conference on Child Labor, Oslo, May.

Deheija, R. H., and R. Gatti. 2001. "Child Labor: The Role of Income Variability and Access to Credit in a Cross Section of Countries." World Bank.

Dessy, S. 2000. "A Defense of Compulsive Measures Against Child Labor." *Journal of Development Economics* 62, no. 1 (June): 261–275.

Dessy, S. E., and S. Pallage. 2001. "Child Labor and Coordination Failures." *Journal of Development Economics* 65, no. 2: 469–476.

Dey-Abbas, J. 1997. "Gender Asymmetry in Intra-Household Resource Allocation in Sub-Saharan Africa." In *Intra-Household Allocations in Developing Countries,* eds. L. Haddad, J. Hoddinot, and H. Alderman. Johns Hopkins University Press.

Doss, C. 2001. "Designing Agricultural Technology for African Woman Farmers: Lessons from 25 Years of Experience." *World Development* 29, no. 12: 2075–2092.

Draper, P., and E. Cashdan. 1988. "Technological Change and Child Behaviors Among the !Kung." *Ethnology: An International Journal of Culture and Social Anthropology:* 339–365.

Eicher, C. K., and D. C. Baker. 1982. "Research on Agricultural Development in Sub-Saharan Africa: A Critical Survey." Michigan State University International Development Paper no. 1.

Eldring, L., S. Nakanyane, and M. Tshoaedi. 2000. "Child Labor in the Tobacco Growing Sector in Africa." Report no. 2000-21. Fafo Institute for Applied Social Sciences.

Fahopunda, E. R.. 1978. "Characteristics of Women Workers in Lagos: Data for Consideration by Labor Market Theorists." *Labor and Society* 3: 158–171.

Fannou-Ako, N., and F. A. Adihou. 1999. "Le trafique des enfants entre le Bénin et le Gabon." Anti-Slavery International.

Farah, D. 2001. "Children of Mali Find Harsh Reality in Ivory Coast Jobs, Young Villagers Seek Escape from Poverty." *Washington Post,* October 7.

Floro, M. S. 1995. "Economic Restructuring, Gender, and the Allocation of Time." *World Development.*

Focus on Africa. 2001. *BBC Journal* (July–September): 33–35.

Frase-Blunt, M. 2002. "The Sugar Daddies' Kiss of Death." *Washington Post,* October 6.

Fratkin, Elliot. 1989. "Household Variation and Gender Inequality in Ariaal Pastoral Production: Results of a Stratified Time-allocation Survey." *American Anthropologist:* 430–440.

Fyfe, A. 1989. *Child Labor.* Polity Press.

Gibbon, P., ed. 1995. *Structural Adjustment and the Working Poor in Zimbabwe.* Uppsala: Nordiska Afrikainstitutet.

Gilborn, L., R. Nyonyintono, R. Kabumbuli, G. Jaggwe-Wadda, and S. Geibel. 2001. "Widows, Orphans, and Property Grabbing: Findings and Solutions from an Intervention Study in Uganda." Paper presented at a Global Health Council conference.

Glick, P., and D. E. Sahn. 1999. "Schooling of Girls and Boys in a West African Country: The Effects of Parental Education." *Economics of Education Review.*

Goldschmidt-Clermont, L. 1994. "Assessing Women's Contributions in Domestic and Related Matters." In *Gender, Work, and Population in Sub-Saharan Africa,* eds. A. Adepoju and C. Oppong. London: ILO.

Gonza, M. J., and P. Moshi. 2002. "Tanzania: Children Working in Commercial Agriculture—Tea: A rapid Assessment." ILO/IPEC.

Graticer, P. L., and L. B. Lerer. 1998 "Child Labor and Health: Quantifying the Global Health Impact of Child Labor." World Bank Education Paper no. 19021.

Grimsrud, B. 2001a. "Measuring and Analyzing Child Labor: Methodological Issues." World Bank Social Protection Discussion Paper no. 0123.

———. 2001b. "What Can Be Done About Child Labor? An Overview of Recent Research and Its Implications for Designing Programs to Reduce Child Labor." World Bank Social Protection Discussion Paper no. 0124.

Grimsrud, B., and L. J. Stokke. 1997. "Child Labour and Institutional Development in Africa: The Case of Egypt and Zimbabwe." Oslo: Fafo Institute for Applied Social Science. Unpublished.

Grootaert, C. 1998. "Child Labor in the Ivory Coast." World Bank Policy Working Paper no. 1905.

Grootaert, C., and R. Kanbur. 1995. "Child Labor: An Economic Perspective." *International Labor Review* 134: 187–203.

Grootaert, C., and H. Patrinos. 2002. "A Four-Country Comparative Study of Child Labor." Paper prepared for the World Bank Conference on Child Labor, Oslo, May.

Hamidou Kane, C. 1961. *L'aventure ambigüe*. Julliard.

Heady, C. 2003. "The Effect of Child Labor on Learning Achievement." *World Development* 31, no 2.

Human Rights Watch Africa. 1997. "Juvenile Injustice: Police Abuse and Detention of Street Children in Kenya." *Human Rights Watch:* 61.

Hunt, P. 1993. "Children's Rights in West Africa: The Case of the Gambia's 'Almudos.'" *Human Rights Quarterly* 15: 499–532.

Hussmann, R., F. Mehran, and V. Verma. 1990. *Surveys of Economically Active Population, Employment, Unemployment, and Underemployment: An ILO Manual on Concepts and Methods.* Geneva: ILO.

ILO (International Labour Organization). 1996a. *Child Labour Surveys: Results of Methodological Experiments in Four Countries, 1992–93.*

―――. 1996b. "Facts and Figures on Child Labor." Pamphlet.

ILO/IPEC (International Labour Organization/International Program for the Eradication of Child Labor). 1997. *Child Labor in Commercial Agriculture in Africa.*

―――. 2004. *Investing in Every Child: An Economic Study of the Costs and Benefits of Eliminating Child Labor.*

ILO/SIMPOC (International Labour Organization/Statistical Information and Monitoring Programme on Child Labour). 2002. "Every Child Counts: New Global Estimates on Child Labor."

Inglehart, R. 1997. *Modernization and Postmodernization: Cultural, Economic, and Political Change in 43 Societies.* Princeton: Princeton University Press.

International Institute of Tropical Agriculture. 2002. "Child Labor in the Cocoa Sector of West Africa: A Synthesis of Findings in Cameroon, Côte d'Ivoire, Ghana, and Nigeria."

Isiugo-Abanihe, U. C. 1985. "Child Fosterage in West Africa." *Population and Development Review* 11, no. 1.

Iversen, V. 2002. "Idiosyncrasies of Child Labor in Peasant Households in Sub-Saharan Africa: Anthropological Observations and the Economics of Labor Obligations and Exchange." Paper presented at the World Bank Conference on Child Labor, Oslo.

Jafarey, S., and S. Lahirib. 2002. "Will Trade Sanctions Reduce Child Labour? The Role of Credit Markets." *Journal of Development Economics* 68, no. 1 (June): 137–156.

Jekinnou, P. 2002. "Artisanat de récupération et de recyclage des déchets métalliques: enjeux et défis." Unpublished manuscript for CIPCRE, Porto-Novo, Bénin.

Jensen, P., and H. Skyt-Nielsen. 1997. "Child Labor or School Attendance? Evidence from Zambia." *Journal of Population Economics* 65: 1049–1054.

Jones, C. 1983. "The Mobilization of Women's Labor for Cash Crop Production: A Game Theoretic Approach." *American Journal of Agricultural Economics.*

Junger, S. 2000. "The Terror of Sierra Leone." *Vanity Fair,* August 2000.

Kadonys, C., M. Madihi, and S. Mtwana. 2002. "Tanzania: Child Labor in the Informal Sector: A Rapid Assessment." ILO/IPEC.

Kamala, E., E. Lusinde, J. Millinga, and J. Mwaitula. 2001. "Tanzania: Children in Prostitution—A Rapid Assessment." ILO/IPEC.

Kamuzora, C. L. 1980. "Constraints to Labour Time Availability in African Smallholder Agriculture: The Case of Bukoba District, Tanzania." *Development and Change* 11, no. 1.

Kayongo-Male, D., and P. Walji. 1984. *Children at Work in Kenya.* Oxford University Press.

Keitetsi, C. 2001. "Mit liv som barnesoldat i Uganda" [My Life as a Child Soldier in Uganda]. Denmark: Ekstrabladets Forlag.

Kielland, A., and R. Ouensavi. 2001. "Le Phénomène des enfants travailleurs migrants du Bénin: Ampleur et determinants." World Bank.

Kielland, A., and I. Sanogo. 2002. "Burkina Faso: Child Labor Migration from Rural Areas—The Magnitude and the Determinants." Terre des Hommes/World Bank.

Kilbride, P., and J. Kilbride. 1993. *Changing Family Life in East Africa.* Nairobi: Gideon S. Were Press.

Kinsey, B., and R. Serra. 2000 "Child Fostering in Rural Zimbabwe." Presentation to the CSAE Conference on Micro-Opportunities in Africa.

Koopman, J. 1992. "The Hidden Roots of the African Food Problem: Looking Within the Rural Household." In Nancy Folbre et al., *Women's Work in the World Economy.* London: Macmillan.

Kopoka, P. A. 2000. "The Problem of Street Children in Africa: An Ignored Tragedy." Paper presented at the International Conference on Street Children's Health in East Africa, Tanzania, 2000.

Kpoghomou, M. 1996. "Travail des enfants dans les mines diamantifères de Friguiagbegare, en Guinée." Paper presented at the UNICEF Regional Conference on the Exploitation of Child Labor in West and Central Africa, Abidjan, July.

Lee Barnes, V., and J. Boddy. 1995. *Aman: The Story of a Somali Girl.* New York: Vintage Books.

Lestaeghe, R. J., ed. 1989. *Reproduction and Social Organization in Sub-Saharan Africa.* Berkeley: University of California Press.

LeVine, R., et al. 1994. *Child Care and Culture: Lessons from Africa.* Cambridge University Press.

Lindahl-Kiessling, K., and H. Landberg, eds. 1994. *Population, Economic Development, and the Environment.* Oxford University Press.

Lloyd, C., and S. Desai. 1992. "Children's Living Arrangements in Developing Countries." *Population Research and Policy Review:* 193–216.

Lloyd, C., and A. Gage-Brandon. 1994. "High Fertility and Children's Schooling in Ghana: Sex Differences in Parental Contributions and Educational Outcomes." *Population Studies* 2: 93–306.

Lloyd, C. B., and A. K. Blanc. 1996. "Children's Schooling in Sub-Saharan Africa: The Role of Fathers, Mothers, and Others." *Population and Development Review* 22: 265–298.

Loewenson, R., and I. Muyaruka. 1992. "Child Labour in Zimbabwe." Report prepared for the government of Zimbabwe and the ILO. October.

Machel, G. 1997. *The Impact of Armed Conflict on Children.* UNICEF.

Marguerat, Y. 2001. "Malheur à la ville dont le prince est un enfant (de la rue)." Text proposed for Cahiers d'Etudes Africaines.

Mason, A. D., and S. R. Khandker. 1998. "Children's Work, Opportunity Cost, and Schooling in Tanzania." Unpublished manuscript prepared for the World Bank.

McGuire, J. S., and B. M. Popkin. 1990. "Helping Women Improve Nutrition in the Developing World." World Bank Technical Paper no. WTP 114.

McKee, L. 1986. "Household Analysis as an Aid to Farming Systems Research: Methodological Issues." In *Understanding Africa's Rural Households and Farming Systems,* ed. J. L. Moock. Boulder: Westview.

McNicoll, G., and M. Cain. 1990. *Rural Development and Population.* Oxford University Press.

Miller, A. 1997. *The Drama of the Gifted Child.* New York: Basic Books.

Moehling, C. 1997. "The Impact of Children's Income on Intra-Household Resource Allocation." Mimeograph. Ohio State University, Department of Economics.

Molo Songololo. 2000. "The Trafficking of Children for the Purpose of Commercial Sexual Exploitation: South Africa." NGO report. Cape Town.

Mott, F. L., and D. Shapiro. 1984. "Seasonal Variation in Labor Force Activity and Intra-Household Substitution of Labor in Rural Kenya." *Journal of Developing Areas* 18: 449–463.

Mueller, E. 1984. "The Value and Allocation of Time in Rural Botswana." *Journal of Development Economics* 15: 329–360.

Munroe, R., R. Munroe, and H. Shimmin. 1984. "Children's Work in Four Cultures: Determinants and Consequences." *American Anthropologist:* 369–379.

Mwami, J. A., A. J. Sanga, and J. Nyoni. 2002. "Tanzania: Child Labor in Mining: A Rapid Assessment." ILO/IPEC.

Nchahaga, G. S. 2002. "Tanzania: Children Working in Commercial Agriculture—Coffee: A Rapid Assessment." ILO/IPEC.

Nelson Mandela Children's Fund. 2001. "A Study into the Situation and Special Needs of Children in Child-Headed Households." Unpublished manuscript. June.

Nkamleu, G. B., and A. Kielland. 2004. "Determinants for Child Labor Participation in Cocoa Farming in Côte d'Ivoire: Task Specificities and Gender Dimensions." World Bank Social Protection Working Paper Series.

Notermans, C. "Fosterage in Cameroon: A Different Social Construction of Motherhood." University of Nijmegen, Department of Anthropology/Center for Women's Studies, Netherlands.

Obbo, C. 1995. "What Women Can Do: AIDS Crisis Management in Uganda." In *Women Wielding the Hoe,* ed. D. F. Bryceson. Oxford: Berg.

Okali, C. "Cocoa and Kinship in Ghana." London: International African Institute and Keagan Paul.

Oloko, Sarah B. A. 1996. "Conceptual Challenges: A Review of Research Findings on the Impact of Child Labor on Child Development, Socialization, Exploitation, and Training." Paper presented at the UNICEF Regional Conference on the Exploitation of Child Labor in West and Central Africa, Abidjan, July.

OMCT (Organisation Mondiale Contre la Torture/World Organization Against Torture). 2001. *Rights of the Child in the Democratic Republic of Congo.*

Onyango, P., et al. 1991a. *A Report on the Nairobi Case Study on Children in Especially Difficult Circumstances.* Nairobi: African Network for the Protection Against Child Abuse and Neglect.

————. 1991b. *Research on Street Children in Kenya.* Nairobi: African Network for the Protection Against Child Abuse and Neglect.

————. 1995. "Towards an International Strategy for the Eradication of Child Labour: In-Depth Country Report." Nairobi: International Working Group on Child Labour.

Ouensavi, R. 2000. "La marginalité urbaine au Bénin: Les nouvelles approches -Cas de la ville de Cotonou." Université Nationale du Bénin des Interfacultaire en Populations et Dynamiques Urbaines.

Parikh, M. 2002. "Slavery in the Yeji Fishing Area." Unpublished report from Ghana mission, Free the Slaves.

Pebley, A., and W. Mbugua. 1989. "Polygyny and Fertility in Sub-Saharan Africa." In *Reproduction and Social Organization in Sub-Saharan Africa,* ed. R. J. Lestaeghe. Berkeley: University of California Press.

Ranjan, P. 1999. "An Economic Analysis of Child Labor." *Economics Letters.*

————. 2001. "Credit Constraints and the Phenomenon of Child Labor." *Journal of Development Economics* 64: 81–102.

Rau, B. 2002. "Child Labor and HIV/AIDS: An Assessment of Policies, Programs, and Projects in South Africa, Tanzania, and Zambia." ILO.

Reynolds, P. 1991. *Dance Civet Cat.* Harare: Baobab Books.

Richards, P., S. Archibald, K. Bah, and J. Vincent. 2003. "Where Have All the Young People Gone? Transitioning Ex-Combatants Towards Community Reconstruction After the War in Sierra Leone." Unpublished report. Wageningen University, Netherlands.

Roberts, P. A., 1988. "Rural Women's Access to Labor in West Africa," In *Patriarchy and Class: African Women in the Home and Work Force,* eds. S. B. Streichter, and J. L. Parpart. Boulder: Westview.

Robinson, W. C. 1992. "Kenya Enters the Fertility Transition." *Population Studies:* 445–457.

Rogers, C. A., and K. A. Swinnerton. 2001. "Inequality, Productivity, and Child Labor: Theory and Evidence." Unpublished paper.

————. 2002a. "Does Child Labor Decrease When Parental Income Rises?" Unpublished paper.

————. 2002b. "A Theory of Exploitative Child Labor." Unpublished paper.

Rogers, G., and G. Standing, eds. 1981. *Child Work, Poverty, and Underdevelopment.* Geneva: ILO.

Rosati, F., and Z. Tzannatos. 2003. "Child Work: An Expository Framework of Altruistic and Non-Altruistic Models." World Bank Social Protection Discussion Paper no. 0305.

Saito, K., H. Mekonnen, and D. Spurling. 1994. "Raising the Productivity of Women Farmers in Sub-Saharan Africa." World Bank Africa Technical Department Series no. 230.

Sall, E. 2000. "Child Labor in Africa: Issues and Perspectives." Paper prepared for Children's Week at the World Bank.

San Martin, O. 1996. "Child Labour and International Trade." Report no. 200. Oslo: Norwegian Institute of International Affairs.

Schildkrout, E. 1981. "The Employment of Children in Kano (Nigeria)." In *Child Work, Poverty, and Underdevelopment,* eds. G. Rodgers and G. Standing. Geneva: ILO.

Sen, A. 1990. "Cooperation, Inequality, and the Family." In *Rural Development and Population,* eds. G. McNicoll and M. Cain. Oxford University Press.

Serra, R. 1996. "An Economic Analysis of Child Fostering in West Africa." PhD diss., University of Cambridge, Christ College.

———. 2000. "A Theoretical Framework for Child Fostering Arrangements in Sub-Saharan Africa." Unpublished paper.

Shapiro, D., and B. Oleko Tambashe. 2001. "Gender, Poverty, Family Structure, and Investments in Children's Education in Kinshasa." *Economics of Education Review.*

Siddiqi, F., and H. A. Patrinos. 1995. "Child Labor: Issues, Causes, and Interventions." HCO Working Paper no. 56. World Bank.

Skjønsberg, E. 1989. *Change in an African Village.* West Hartford, Conn.: Kumarian Press.

Soumonni, E. 2000. "Les règles traditionnelles du placement d'enfants au Bénin." Keynote speech presented at the World Bank Conference on Child Protection, Abomey, Benin.

Staudt, K. 1987. "Uncaptured or Unmotivated? Women and the Food Crisis in Africa." *Rural Sociology* 52, no. 1: 37–55.

Subbarao, K., A. Mattimore, and K. Plangemann. 2001. "Social Protection of Africa's Orphans and Vulnerable Children." World Bank, Africa Region.

Suda, C. 1993. "Baseline Survey on Street Children in Nairobi." Unpublished report. October.

Tadaro, M. 1988. "Family Structure, Implicit Contracts, and the Demand for Children in Southern Nigeria." *Population and Development Review* 14: 571–594.

Teffera, T., and T. Fisseha. 2001. "Child Labor in Ethiopia: Its Conditions and Link with Early Childhood Education." Unpublished report. Addis Ababa, March 2001.

Thomas, J. J. 1992. *Informal Economic Activity.* New York: Harvester Wheatsheaf.

Thorner, D., B. Kerblay, and R. Smith. 1966. *Chayanov and the Theory of Peasant Economy.* R. D. Irwin.

Tørres, L. 2000. "The Smoking Business: Tobacco Workers in Malawi." Report no. 339. Fafo Institute for Applied Social Science.

Tovo, M. 1995. "Equatorial Guinea: The Politics of Poverty." Unpublished manuscript prepared for the World Bank. February.

Udry, C. 1996. "Gender, Agricultural Production, and the Theory of the Household." *Journal of Political Economy* 104, no. 5: 1010–1046.

Udry, C., J. Hoddinott, H. Alderman, and L. Haddad. 1995. "Gender Differentials in Farm Productivity: Implications for Household Efficiency." *Food Policy.*

UNDP (United Nations Development Programme). 1998. "Enquête sur l'emploi du temps au Bénin." Cotonou, Benin.

UNICEF (United Nations Children's Fund). 1994. "Les enfants vidomegon, les enfants et rupture, les enfants abandonnés au Bénin." Benin.

———. 1998. "Study on Special Child Protection Issues in Twelve Countries of West and Central Africa." Abidjan, Côte d'Ivoire.

———. 1999a. "Child Domestic Work." *Innocenti Digest* 5.

———. 1999b. "Le traffic international des enfants dans le Sud Bénin." UNICEF Benin and Service Diocesain de Développement et Action Caritative.

————. 2002. "Child Trafficking in West Africa: Policy Responses." Florence: Innocenti Research Center.

————. 2004. *State of the World's Children.*

UNICEF (United Nations Children's Fund), UNAIDS (Joint United Nations Programme on HIV/AIDS), and USAID (US Agency for International Development). 2004. *Children on the Brink 2004: A Joint Report on New Orphan Estimates and a Framework for Action.* New York. Available online at http://www.unicef.org or http://www.usaid.gov.

US Department of Labor. *By the Sweat and Toil of Children.* 6 vols.

Walker, W. 1998. "A Visual Poverty Assessment: Burkina Faso." World Bank.

Weir, S. 2000. "Concealed Preferences: Parental Attitudes to Education and Enrollment Choice in Rural Ethiopia."

Weisner, T. S., C. Bradley, and P. L. Kilbride. 1997. "African Families and the Crisis of Social Change."

Wenger, M. 1989. "Work, Play, and Social Relationships Among Children in a Giriama Community." In *Children's Social Networks and Supports,* ed. Deborah Belle. New York: John Wiley and Sons.

Whitehead, A. 1994. "Wives and Mothers: Female Farmers in Africa." In *Gender, Work, and Population in Sub-Saharan Africa,* eds. A. Adepoju and C. Oppong. London: ILO.

Whiteside, M. 1999. "*Ganyu* Labor in Malawi and Its Implications for Livelihood Security Interventions." Oxford International Programme in Malawi.

Whiting, B., and J. Whiting. 1975. *Children of Six Cultures: A Psychocultural Analysis.* Cambridge: Harvard University Press.

World Bank. 1994. "Benin: Toward a Poverty Alleviation Strategy." Report no. 12706-BEN. Population and Human Resources Division, Occidental and Central Africa Department, August 5.

————. 1996. "Togo: Overcoming the Crisis, Overcoming Poverty." Report no. 15526-TO. Population and Human Resources Operations Division, West Central Africa Department, Africa Region, June 25.

————. 1998. "Ethiopia." Social Sector Note Report no. 16860—ET. Human Development, Eastern and Southern Africa, Africa Region, February 27.

————. 2001. "Addressing Child Labor in the Workplace and Supply Chain." IFC Good Practice Note.

Index

Abanya, Concy, 116
Abilities and demand, balance between, 131
Ableidinger, Joseph, 47, 48
Accidents as consequences of child labor, 128–129
African Charter on the Rights and Welfare of the Child, 8, 10
African Union, 8
Age-earning curves, 141–142
Age of maturity, debate over legal, 1–2
Agriculture: commercial labor market, 91–94; consequences of child labor, 126–127; ruralization and child labor, 25–27; subsistence, 61–64; urban culture clashing with rural farming society, 6–7, 17
AIDS (acquired immune deficiency syndrome): consequences of child labor, 127; orphans, 31, 45, 49; sexual abuse of children, 136, 138; and sexual abuse between teachers and students, 112, 136; virgin, belief in prevention through sex with a, 112–113
Alcoholism in homes affecting child domestic workers, 30
Alliance fostering, 31
Angola, 40, 113

Apprenticeship arrangement, child labor as: consequences of child labor, 126–127; construction sites, 83–85; fishing, 82–83; fostering arrangements, 31, 32; garages, 77–79; overview, 75–77; tailoring, 79–82; talibés, 84, 86–88
Assets as child labor–saving/demanding, 61

Baifa people, 136
Bales, Kevin, 42, 97
Bars/restaurants, children working in, 102–103
Bass, Loretta, 29
Beauchemin, Eric, 116
Belgium, 40
Benin: agriculture and commercial labor market, 92; common work activities of children, 58–59; cures for child labor, 156, 157; fostering arrangements, 34; talibés, 86, 87; trafficking, child, 37
Beti people, 136
Bhalotra, Sonia, 17, 21–22
Black, Maggie, 96
Bolsa Escola program (Brazil), 150–151
Botswana: agriculture and commercial

About the Book

IN THIS ACCESSIBLE TREATMENT OF CHILD LABOR IN AFRICA, STRAIGHT-forward prose is enriched throughout with photographs that give a human face to the issues involved.

The authors draw on sources ranging from scholarly studies to children's own voices. After providing a general background to the topic—debunking myths in the process—they describe the work typically done by African children in the home, as apprentices, and in commercial labor markets. They also present a clearheaded discussion of the worst, exploitive kinds of child labor. The book ends with a discussion of the effects of work on children, suggesting a variety of concrete, realistic approaches to minimizing negative consequences.

Anne Kielland consults with the World Bank, nongovernmental organizations, and corporations in the area of child protection. Her pioneering work includes large-scale studies of the labor migration of children in West Africa and the role of children in household risk management. **Maurizia Tovo** is on the staff of the World Bank, where she is a social protection specialist for West Africa and coordinates the Orphans and Vulnerable Children Thematic Group.